colorful FABRIC collage

SKETCH·FUSE·QUILT!

SUE BLEIWEISS

INTERWEAVE.
interweave.com

For Iris, because Mistyfuse made it possible!

ACKNOWLEDGMENTS

A huge thank you to Deborah Boschert, Barb Forrister, Leslie Tucker Jenison, Lyric Kinard, Jamie Fingal, Kathy Sperino, Desiree Habicht, Kathy York, and Terri Stegmiller for contributing original artwork to this book. I also owe a huge debt of gratitude to my editor, Leslie O'Neill, for her superior editing skills as well as all of her feedback, guidance, and help in refining not only the written manuscript but also the projects in it.

Thanks also to Sherry and Larry for their kind words, encouragement, and positive feedback about my work. Finally, thank you to my husband Scott, whose love and support mean more to me than words can ever express.

© 2014 Sue Bleiweiss
Photography © 2014 Interweave,
a division of F+W Media, Inc.

Interweave
A division of F+W Media, Inc.
4868 Innovation Dr.
Fort Collins, CO 80525-5576
interweave.com

Manufactured in China by
RR Donnelley Shenzhen

Library of Congress Cataloging-in-
Publication Data

Bleiweiss, Sue, author.
 Colorful fabric collage : sketch, fuse,
quilt! / Sue Bleiweiss.
   pages cm
 Includes index.
 ISBN 978-1-62033-692-2 (pbk.)
 ISBN 978-1-62033-693-9 (PDF)
 1. Quilting. 2. Color in textile crafts.
 I. Title.
 TT835.B5125 2015
 746.46--dc23

 2014031631

EDITOR
Leslie T. O'Neill

TECHNICAL EDITOR
Kerry Smith

PHOTOGRAPHER
Ann Swanson

ILLUSTRATOR
Missy Shepler

STYLIST
Katie Himmelberg

ASSOCIATE ART DIRECTOR
Charlene Tiedemann

COVER AND INTERIOR DESIGNER
Karla Baker

LAYOUT AND PRODUCTION DESIGNER
Bekah Thrasher

table of
contents

Introduction:

why i choose
TO FUSE

The first quilt I ever made was a traditionally pieced nine-patch block quilt with a flying geese border. It was a small quilt, but it took me a long time to finish it. I was so obsessed with getting all of those ¼-inch (6 mm) seams and corners to line up exactly right. By the time I was finished, I swore I'd never make another quilt again—I just didn't enjoy the process. And I really hated having to follow directions.

I put away all of the fabric and the quilting tools. I focused on creating books and journals and three-dimensional objects such as boxes and vessels. But it wasn't long until I found myself wanting to explore working on flat surfaces and creating work that I could hang on my walls.

I started dabbling in creating fused fabric collage art quilts. Fusing gave me the freedom to create quilts without having to worry about lining up corners or intersections and whether or not my seams were straight. With fusing, no shape is off limits! Circles, arcs, wavy edges, or pieces with sharp corners are difficult to piece, but they are a snap to fuse. Fusing gives me the power to create a quilt that depicts any realistic or abstract imagery that I can dream up with no worries about how I will put it together.

Find Your Inner Art Quilter

I have two goals with *Colorful Fabric Collage*. The first is to help you discover how versatile fusing can be beyond just using it to adhere one piece of fabric to another. I've created a wide range of quilted projects, from art quilts to hang on your walls to personal accessories that accent your life with creativity.

Each project uses fusing as a primary part of the creative process as well as the construction process. You can recreate the projects exactly how I have

presented them, but I encourage you to personalize them to your own style. Use them as a springboard. Create them using the fabrics, colors, and imagery that you like to work with.

My second goal is to show you that fusing can help you make that transition to becoming an art quilter just as easily as I did. Once you add a layer of fusible web to the back of your fabrics, there's no image you can't recreate. If you can imagine it, you can turn it into an art quilt.

When you fuse a piece of fabric that is cut on an arc, you don't have to be concerned about puckers or gaps—you can break free from the restrictions of straight seams and corners that must align. Maybe you have photos from your garden, a trip abroad, or even of your pets that you'd like to recreate in an art quilt. Using fusing as your construction method makes it possible!

Inspiration Is Everywhere

This book also shares with you nine inspiring art quilts created by some of my favorite fiber artists who use fusing as an integral part of their creative process. As you read about how each of these artists incorporates fusible webbing in their art quilts, let your mind wander. Think about how you might want to explore the use of fused fabrics in your art quilts.

Remember, with fusing no shape is impossible—your only limit is your own imagination. The more you explore and experiment, the more you will discover and learn. So grab some fusible web and some quilting fabrics and let your creative imagination run wild!

I wish you all the best in your creative endeavors!

CHAPTER one

dream it!

Making the transition from traditional quilter to art quilter is easier than you think. If you've been making traditional quilts, then you probably have almost all of the tools and supplies you need in your studio already. The difference is in how you use them.

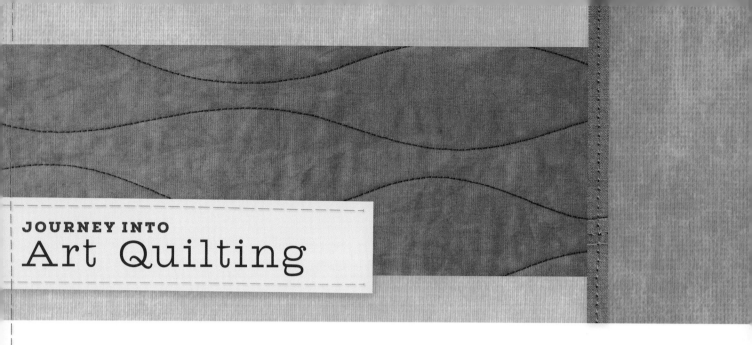

JOURNEY INTO
Art Quilting

The steps to create an art quilt are essentially no different than those used to sew a traditional quilt, but the outcome is vastly different. Instead of assembling a top sewn from well-known blocks, you create a quilt from any image you dream up. Sketch your idea, choose your colors and fabrics, and then head into your sewing space to begin the construction process.

The two most important tools that I use in my art quilt-making process are my sketchbook and a pencil. Every single quilt comes to life on the pages of my sketchbook. Now, I know that some of you are shaking your head and thinking that using a sketchbook is not for you because you can't draw, or you think it's easier and faster to just jump in and start cutting and fusing fabric. I urge you—really, I'm begging you!—to just give working on paper first a try.

Sketching gives you the opportunity to fully explore your ideas before you begin the quilt-making process. It will save you a lot of time, wasted fabric, and false starts, and you'll enjoy actually making your quilt a lot more.

Start with an Idea

All of the ideas for my quilts start on paper as rough sketches done in either pencil or with a fine-point black marker. I like to work in an unlined sketchbook that lies flat when opened, but you might find it easier to work on individual pieces of paper. Your paper doesn't have to be anything fancy—a stack of printer paper will work just fine if that's what you have available.

Sometimes, before I start sketching or drawing, I make a list of words associated with the idea for my quilt. This helps me brainstorm the imagery I might want to include in the quilt. It is particularly helpful when I'm creating a quilt with recognizable imagery, such as the City Skyline Art Quilt (page 76). My list of words for City Skyline was "buildings, windows, doors, clouds, antennas, billboard, sky, planes, and birds."

If I'm creating a quilt that is made up of geometric shapes with no realistic or stylized imagery, I skip this step and just begin sketching.

SKETCHING TIP *Stuck for an idea? Take a look out the window and make a list of what you see: birds, mailboxes, trees, a sunset, a garden, cars whizzing by, a city street, the chicken coop, a bicycle, the doghouse, a butterfly, or a wintry landscape. All of these would make terrific subjects for an art quilt.*

Once you have your list of words, you can start doing some rough sketches. Keep your sketches simple and free of details. There's no need to get fancy with your sketches! Stick with line drawings and don't worry about including every tiny little detail. Just get an initial idea of what you want the quilt to look like down on paper while you start thinking about what size you want your quilt to be. Don't worry about making that first sketch (or any of your sketches) perfect or to scale. Think of your sketches as your own private, visual playground. Nobody but you has to see them. Sketching is your opportunity to shape and refine your ideas before you start cutting into any fabric.

I like to start my sketches by drawing a box on the page in the shape of what I think the quilt will look like: square or rectangle, landscape or portrait. This gives me a framework to work in and a guide that helps determine the shapes that the images on the quilt will take.

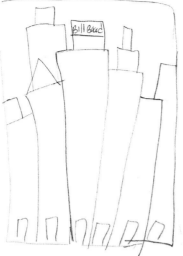

add color to your sketches to get a better feel for your final quilt design.

I might do several different drawings of my quilt, changing and refining the images that I include. Sometimes, I will draw some of the elements on their own to work out how I want them to look.

After I've gotten some good rough sketches on paper, sometimes the black-and-white drawing doesn't give me a clear enough picture of what the quilt will look like. That's when I like to go back and include color using colored pencils. If you want to retain your original black-and-white sketch, make copies of it and then add color to the copies. This lets you try out different color combinations.

Think Big, Draw Bigger

When I'm happy with my sketch, I make a full-sized drawing of it to work from. I do this no matter how large or small the quilt will be. While it's true that the sketch is a good representation of what I want my quilt to look like, it may not always translate perfectly into fabric without making some changes to the scale of the images.

This is particularly true of a really large quilt that is several yards or meters wide by several yards or meters tall. A 6-inch-square (15 cm) sketch of that same quilt doesn't really give an accurate feel for the amount of space that I'll fill with imagery. My full-sized drawing gives me an opportunity to change the scale of the images, add or remove elements, and move things around to better fill the amount of space I'll ultimately work with.

However, I don't always include all of the small details in my full-sized drawings. For instance, I did not draw all of the windows in the City Skyline Art Quilt. I knew that I'd cut all of them out by hand, so I didn't need to take the time to draw them all in.

I like to preserve each of my original scale drawings. I can refer back to them while I'm constructing the quilt, and in case I want to make another version of the quilt in a different color, I still have my templates. Once I'm happy with the drawing, I make a tracing of it that I will cut up and use as patterns when I cut the fabric versions of my images.

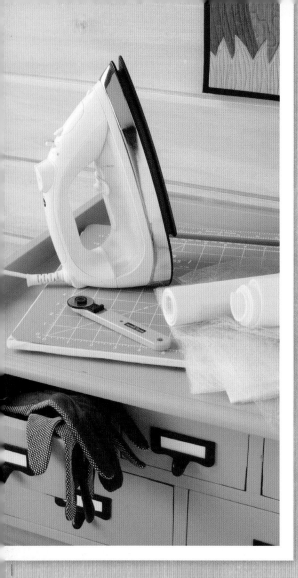

The Necessities: Art Quilt Tools and Materials

The tools and materials you use in your studio will depend on your personal preferences. I encourage you to try many different brands and sizes of various tools to determine the ones you like best.

Keep your tools and supplies clean and in good working order. Nothing is more frustrating than trying to cut fabric with a dull rotary blade or trying to get a straight cut with a warped ruler.

Fusible web: Fusible web is not only my absolute favorite tool for making art quilts, it is also the most important. It's the foundation of my construction process. Many different brands of fusible web are available. My fusible web of choice is Mistyfuse because it doesn't add any bulk or stiffness to my pieces. It is a particularly lightweight, solvent-free fusible web, and it stays soft and creates a strong bond.

This is especially important to my construction process—when I build a piece, I can end up with upward of seven or eight layers of fabric fused together, which I need to be able to stitch through. Using a lightweight fusible web ensures that I can stitch easily through all of those layers as well as avoid fusible glue building up on my needles.

Most fusible web brands come with a release paper, but Mistyfuse does not.

I used Mistyfuse fusible web to make all of the projects in this book. It is available in packages that each contain 2½ yards (2.3 meters) of 20-inch-wide (51 cm) web.

Pressing sheet: When working with a non-paper-backed fusible web, you need to use a pressing sheet to protect the sole plate of your iron from the fusible glue. You can use either a Teflon-coated sheet or a piece of baking parchment paper. Whatever you use, do not use freezer paper! Because it does not have a silicone coating, freezer paper will adhere to the fusible web.

Irons: In my studio, I use a dry iron because I rarely use steam on my art quilts. This type of iron does not produce steam, so the sole plate does not have any steam holes in it. On the few occasions when I want to use steam, I use a spray mister filled with tap water to lightly spray the surface I want to press, let it sit for a moment, and then iron with a hot iron.

For some projects, a mini iron can be helpful also, such as when fusing small, narrow pieces of fabric.

Cutting tools: Rotary cutters come in several different sizes and handle types, none more suited to making fusible fabric collages than any other. I keep a range of sizes on hand, from 28mm to 60mm, as well as a stock of replacement blades for each.

To achieve nice, straight, consistently measured cuts, you'll need an acrylic ruler designed for use with a rotary cutter. These also come in many different sizes and shapes, but for straight cuts I use either a 6-inch by 24-inch (15 by 61 cm) or a 3-inch by 18-inch (7.5 by 45.5 cm) ruler, depending on the size of the piece of fabric that I am cutting.

I often prefer to cut shapes for my projects using scissors. For those projects, I use scissors with a serrated blade because it helps to grip the fabric as I cut. This results in less stress on my hand and a more precise cut.

The middle layer: Choosing the right quilt batting depends on the materials you prefer, the feel you want your quilt to have, and what your budget will allow. Each type has pros and cons to consider.

Synthetic polyester battings are inexpensive, and they are generally lighter in weight than cotton or wool. The resulting quilt won't have much drape. However, polyester battings have a tendency to beard; fibers from the batting work their way through to the surface of the quilt. They're also not a good choice for projects such as hot plate mats or quilted potholders that will be exposed to heat.

Batting made from 100 percent cotton creates a warm quilt with nice drape. It is not prone to bearding. However, it may shrink anywhere from three to five percent, which can create an undesirable puckered effect in your washed quilt.

Wool batting is lightweight, soft, and also has a nice drape. But it can be costly and, as with all wool products, it can attract moths.

Silk batting is a good choice for quilted garments because of its lightweight body and drape; but it, too, can be expensive.

Another option is a batting made from a blend of fibers. Using a blend typically gives you a combination of the pros and cons of each fiber, and the batts are usually less expensive than using a 100 percent natural fiber batting.

Of course, because this is art quilting, you can choose an appropriately unconventional material for your middle layer, too. For my art quilts that will hang on a wall, I prefer to use wool felt instead of traditional quilt batting as my middle layer. For all of the art quilt projects in this book, I used wool felt, but you can use any type of batting that you prefer.

I especially like National Nonwovens WoolFelt, which is a blend of 35 percent wool and 65 percent rayon. It adds body without adding any loft, and I like the way my quilts hang as a result. It will shrink, so it should be laundered the same way your project will be washed before you use it. When I use it for my art quilts, I do not wash it because the finished quilt will not be laundered.

WoolFelt is usually folded and then rolled around the bolt, which can cause wrinkles and creases. To remove these before you use it, lay it out on your ironing surface, spritz it with water, and iron with a hot iron. You may have to repeat this a couple of times on both sides to steam out any creases.

When you want to add stiffness to certain craft projects, such as journals or tote bags, consider combining quilt batting or wool felt with a layer of stiff interfacing, such as Peltex 70, Stiffy, or Timtex. These interfacings add stability and strength and are easy to sew through with your sewing machine.

General Sewing Tools

I have two sewing machines in my studio: a traditional, standard BERNINA 750 QE, which can sew a variety of stitches using a pressure foot as well as handle free-motion stitching; and a Handi Quilter Sweet Sixteen sit-down, long-arm machine, which is for free-motion stitching only. I prefer to use the long-arm machine for quilting only really large quilts.

All of the projects in this book can be completed using a standard home sewing machine. If you want to incorporate free-motion quilting techniques in your quilts or projects, refer to your sewing machine's user guide for setting information.

Keep your sewing machine clean and free of dust. After each large project, I remove the bobbin and presser footplate and clean out any lint and dust. Consult your machine's manual to learn where and how often your machine needs to be oiled.

Whatever sewing machine you use, be sure to keep a supply of needles on hand. For my standard machine, I prefer to use Schmetz brand needles because of their reliable quality and availability. It's important to use the right needle for the project and fabrics that you are working on to ensure success. Schmetz provides this information on its website. The company also has a comprehensive iPhone and iPad app with everything you need to know about choosing the right needle for your fabric.

In general, most sewing machine needles should be changed after eight to twelve hours of sewing. But that is not a hard and fast rule. If you've used your needle to sew through nontraditional mixed media materials, such as paper or metal mesh, you should change your needle more frequently—those surfaces will dull your needle quickly.

What's the best way to tell if it's time to change your needle or if you are using the correct one? Look at your stitches. Consider how your machine is performing. If there are uneven stitches and a lot of thread breaks, first try changing the needle.

You may find it easier to free-motion stitch if you are wearing a pair of nonslip gloves. I like to clip the tops of the fingers off of the gloves so that I can perform nimble tasks, such as changing the bobbin or machine thread, without having to take them off.

When you're buying thread, the most important thing to remember is to get the best quality you can find. Those cheap bargain-bin ten-spools-for-a-dollar threads are not really the bargain they appear to be—they are always made from inferior materials and will break and shred when used. You may also see color variations within a spool as you sew.

Threads come in several different weights. A thread's weight is determined by how many kilometers of it equals one kilogram. So a 40-weight thread means that 40 kilometers of it weighs 1 kilogram. The higher the number, the thinner the thread. Any thread 30 weight or higher can be used in the top of your machine. I generally work with threads by Gutermann, Aurifil, and Superior Threads, and I keep a wide range of colors and types on hand in my studio so that no matter what color fabric I'm ready to start quilting on, I have a coordinating thread for it.

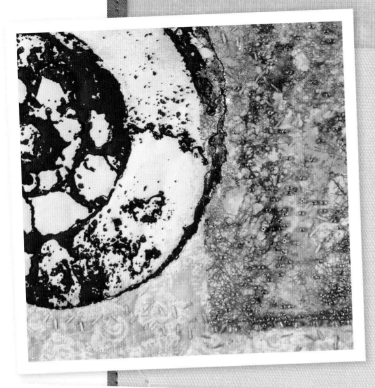

inspired by
cloth

I created the projects in this book using my hand-dyed solid cottons and commercially available batiks, but that doesn't mean you have to. You may not be interested in dyeing or painting your own fabric to use in your art quilts, and that's okay. You may have a fondness for small-scale prints, paisleys, retro images, or plaids—go right ahead and use them in your work. Or maybe you have a stash of silk, linen, velvet, or denim that you'd like to work with. Just because the word "quilt" appears in the description of your work, it doesn't mean that you're limited to working with only traditional cotton quilting fabric.

Look no further than the nine spotlight guest artists for examples of using both traditional and nontraditional materials to create art quilts. These 12" × 12" (30.5 × 30.5 cm) works are scattered throughout this book. They exemplify a variety of fusing techniques and represent very different points of view. The most important rule to remember when choosing fabric is there is no rule! Each art quilter has to find her own style, so I encourage you to experiment and work with whatever types of fabric appeal to you.

Ammonite VIII (detail)
by Lyric Kinard

Welcome (detail)
by Kathy York

CHAPTER two

dye it!

With the rainbow of commercially available solid quilting cottons waiting on the shelves of the fabric store, you are no doubt wondering why you might dye your own. The answer is simple: It's easy, fun, and creative. You can take plain white fabric, dye it to the exact colors of your imagination, and then make the quilt you've sketched from thin air.

Peacock Blue
D 62

Grape
D 117

Dragon fruit
224 G04
G

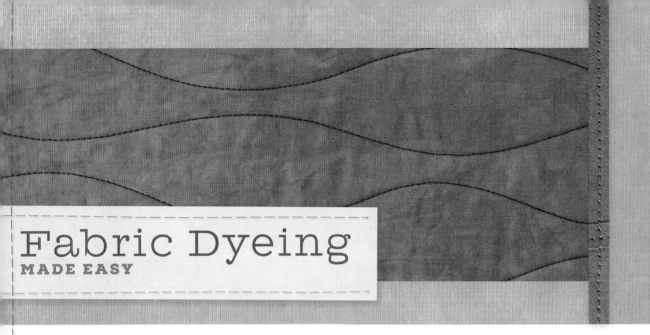

Fabric Dyeing
MADE EASY

Despite the dizzying array of commercial fabrics available to quilters today, I prefer to work primarily with fabrics that I've dyed myself in a range of vibrant candy-colored hues. They give me more control over my color palette as well as continuity across my work. The imagery changes from each quilt to the next, but my rich, jewel-tone color palette stays fairly consistent. It's become the hallmark of my signature style.

After several years of dyeing cotton fabric to use in my art quilts, I've developed an easy, straightforward method that anyone can do. It uses Procion dye and a small amount of water and soda ash.

I prefer to create my art quilts using only my solid-colored, hand-dyed fabrics, but I will add in a batik fabric where I want to add some subtle patterning. I like that when I cut into a batik fabric I have swaths of color across the surface, leaving the actual imagery of the batik undefined. This makes it easy to combine with my hand-dyed fabric because the imagery on the fabric doesn't become a focal point that detracts from the overall visual impact of the finished quilt.

DYEING TIP *All supplies used for dyeing should never be used for any other purpose.*

To dye your own fabrics, you'll need these easy-to-find-online supplies:

Procion dyes: These are cold-water, fiber-reactive dyes. They will bond to the fibers of plant-based fabrics, such as cotton, linen, silk, and rayon, without the use of steam. They are light-fast and washable. The only chemical that you need to fix them to the surface of the cloth is soda ash.

Procion dyes are available in a wide range of premixed colors. That's how I prefer to buy them, so that I don't have to mix my own from primary colors.

Dye powders: Dye powders are packaged in jars ranging from 2 ounces to 25 pounds. A 2 ounce jar contains approximately 20 to 25 teaspoons of dye, which is enough to dye several yards of fabric, depending on how dark you like your colors.

Store unused dye powders in a cool, dry place. They will remain useable for several years, although they will gradually weaken over time.

Respirator: To protect yourself from breathing in dye particles, you must always wear a respirator when working with dye powders.

Soda ash: Soda ash permanently fixes the dye to the fiber molecules. Soda ash is available in bags of 1 pound to 50 pounds.

Because I do a lot of dyeing on a regular basis, I buy it in 25 pound bags. To get started with dyeing, a 1-pound or 2-pound bag will be plenty. Store it in an airtight container in a cool, dry place and it will last indefinitely.

Plastic zip bags: 1 gallon- or 2 gallon-sized bags work great. You'll use these to soak your fabric in the dye solution.

Rubber gloves: I like to use long rubber gloves, such as those for washing dishes. Make sure both of the gloves are in good condition and that they do not have holes in them. When you reach into the zip bag to manipulate the dyed fabric, you won't have to worry about dyeing your arms.

Plastic sheeting: It's important to cover your work surfaces to protect them from the chemicals and any spilled dye used during the dyeing sessions.

Measuring spoons and cups: Use a permanent marker to mark them so that you don't mix them up with the ones you use for cooking.

Coffee filters: Use them to strain your dye mixture to screen out any undissolved dye particles, which will cause speckling on the fabric.

Glass jars with tight-fitting lids: You'll use them to mix the powdered dyes with water. Pick jars, such as old pickle jars, that are large enough to hold at least one cup of water.

Large bucket: Choose a 5 gallon (18.9 L) bucket. This will give you plenty of room to soak several yards of fabric in several gallons of water. It's a manageable size that doesn't get too heavy when filled with water and fabric.

Shout Color Catcher sheets: When you wash your dyed fabrics in the washing machine, just toss one sheet into the load to keep any excess dye from traveling onto other fabrics.

Fabric: If you're using Procion dyes, choose any plant-based fabric, including cotton. Make sure it's marked PFD (prepared for dyeing). Otherwise, you will need to prewash all your fabric in hot water without fabric softener to remove any sizing before it can be dyed.

> **DYEING TIP** *Procion dyes pose no airborne health hazard once they are mixed with water. When the dyes are in powdered form, it is imperative not to breathe them in. You must wear a respirator or a mask before you open any of the containers. DO NOT do this in front of a fan or an open window. Close the containers as soon as you finish pouring out the dye. Do this away from other people and pets.*

HAND-DYED FABRIC
GLASS JARS
MEASURING CUP AND SPOONS
SODA ASH
DYE POWDERS
COFFEE FILTERS
SHOUT COLOR CATCHER SHEETS
RUBBER GLOVES, LARGE BUCKET, RESPIRATOR

Four Steps to
Dye Fabric

Even if you've never dyed fabric before, you'll be able to dye fabric successfully the first time using my method. As with any new technique, it takes time to master reproducing consistent results because of the differences in fabric types, water quality, and dye colors and measurements. This is why it's so important to keep notes and experiment with small pieces before dyeing large quantities of yardage—but it's also part of the fun of exploring the technique. Although your results may not be what you initially expected, you'll probably find that some of your most exciting pieces will be the result of happy accidents and serendipity.

Step 1: Soak the fabric in a solution of soda ash and water

1. Fill the 5 gallon (18.9 L) bucket with several gallons of warm water. Add ½ cup (120 ml) of soda ash for each gallon (3.8 L) of water.

2. Cut or tear your fabric into manageable-sized pieces that will fit comfortably in zip bags. I work with either ½ yard (45.5 cm) or 1 yard (91.5 cm) pieces.

3. Add the fabric to the bucket. Let it soak in the soda ash and water solution for at least twenty minutes before you dye it.

Step 2: Mix the dye

1. To mix the dye, put approximately ¼ to ½ cup (60 to 120 ml) of warm water in the jar and add 1 teaspoon (5 ml) of dye powder. The water should be warm, not hot. Screw the lid on tightly and shake it really well to dissolve the dye powder.

   When I mix dyes, I use a ratio of 1 teaspoon (5 ml) of dye to 1 cup (240 ml) of water. This results in a rich, vibrant color. My ratio is not a hard and fast rule—you can adjust the amount of dye you add to the water to get lighter or darker tones.

   How do you know how much dye to use to get the color you want? That knowledge comes from lots of experimenting and experience. Keep notes and make many samples so that when you find the formula that gives you the result you want, you can recreate it.

   Whenever I dye a piece of fabric with a new color, I write the dye color on a piece of Tyvek with a black permanent marker, and I stitch the Tyvek to the fabric. This makes it easy to identify the fabric when it comes out of the dryer with all of the other fabrics. After I've pressed the fabric, I cut off a small swatch and staple it to a card with notes about how much dye, water, and fabric I used to achieve that result.

   The only exception I make to my dye formula is when I work with black dye. To get a nice, rich black fabric, I add 2 tablespoons (30 ml) of dye to 1 cup (240 ml) of water, and then I dye the fabric twice. After the fabric comes out of the washing machine, I mix a second dye bath and dye it again.

2. Strain the mixed dye through a coffee filter into a measuring cup, and add enough water to bring the mixture to 1 cup (240 ml). This step is optional; however, I recommend it because it prevents any undissolved dye particles from coming into contact with your fabric.

Step 3: Soak the fabric in the dye

1. Take a piece of the wet fabric, after soaking in the soda ash solution for at least twenty minutes, and squeeze out the excess water. Add the fabric to a zip bag, pour in the strained dye, and knead the bag to distribute the dye. Now there's nothing to do but wait and let the dye do its job.

   Let your fabric soak in the dye for a minimum of four hours. Knead the bag occasionally to distribute the dye throughout the cloth as it sits in the bag. The more you knead the bag, the more evenly dyed the surface of your fabric will be.

   You can let your fabric pieces soak longer than four hours—I have even let my fabric sit in dye overnight in plastic bags.

Step 4: Rinse the fabric and press

1. After the fabric pieces have soaked long enough, pull them out of the bags and give them a quick rinse and squeeze to remove any excess water. Make sure you wear your rubber gloves!

   I don't bother to rinse them until the water runs clear because I'd be at the sink forever.

2. Toss the fabrics into the washer along with a Shout Color Catcher sheet and wash them with regular detergent. Wash like colors together—don't put the blues and greens in with the pinks and yellows.

3. Then toss them in the dryer to dry them. Give them a nice press with a hot iron, and they're ready to be used in your next fused and stitched creation.

Tone-on-Tone Fabrics

Although most of my work is created using solid fabrics, I also like to work with tone-on-tone hand-dyed fabrics that I've made using Jacquard Color Magnet and Thermofax silk screens. Color Magnet is a dye attractant available as a liquid in a jar or a pen. It attracts more dye where it is applied, so those areas are dyed a darker hue. Once the dye attractant has dried on the surface of the cloth, the fabric is immersed in a dye bath. The result is a beautiful, one-of-a-kind, tone-on-tone fabric.

My favorite way to apply Color Magnet to the fabric is by screen-printing with the pourable liquid. You can also apply it to fabric by stamping it, stenciling it, and even squirting it with a craft syringe. I like to use Thermofax silkscreens, which are made from a durable plastic mesh. You can buy them online from several artists, some of whom will even make custom silkscreens from your drawings.

I work on a lightly padded surface of two layers of wool felt when I screen print. Place your fabric on top of a padded surface and your silkscreen on top of the fabric. Screen your images from the center of the fabric to the edges.

Spoon some Color Magnet along the top edge of the silkscreen and then, using a squeegee held at a 45-degree angle, drag the liquid across the screen. I usually make two or three passes across the screen to make sure the Color Magnet has permeated the screen image and the fabric. You'll notice that the Color Magnet will look yellow on your fabric, but it will not change the color of the dye you use. The yellow coloring is just to make it easy to see the prints on the fabric as you are working.

To create a repeated pattern, carefully lift the screen off of the fabric and place it down in another area. Repeat the process until the fabric is entirely covered with the image. Hang the fabric to dry completely before adding it to a dye bath. Don't let the Color Magnet dry on the surface of your silkscreens as it may clog the screen.

PRINTING TIP *If you're worried about laying the screen down on top of a wet area, you can wait for the fabric to dry before screening more images.*

Kathy Sperino

One of my favorite things to do is to find and incorporate nontraditional materials into my art. In this piece, I used a stack of used Shout Color Catcher sheets that had been tossed in the washer when I was washing out newly dyed fabric.

No two sheets were the same color. I applied Mistyfuse fusible web to one side of several blue sheets and then cut them into scraps. I pressed the scraps to a piece of muslin and then stitched the muslin to a base fabric. I cut the blue base piece apart and stitched in strips of purple-dyed Color Catchers to create the reeds. Green-dyed Color Catchers were cut in half lengthwise and fused to one another end to end to obtain the length I needed. The dragonfly is a craft straw covered with a piece of fused silk ribbon along with fused layers of cheesecloth. I used bridal illusion tulle to create the wings.

Most of my work is inspired from nature found around my home, in my memories, or in my photos. I created this piece during the dead of winter from daydreams of long, hot, summer days sitting by my fish pond.

Purple Reeds
12" × 12" (30.5 × 30.5 cm)

CHAPTER three

fuse it!

Fusible web isn't just for adhering appliqué shapes to your quilt tops. You can use it in your sewing in many different ways: to interface delicate fabrics, baste a quilt easily and efficiently, create color shading effects and textures, and more.

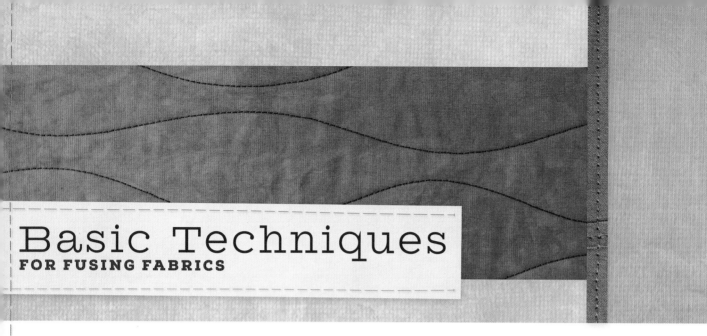

Basic Techniques
FOR FUSING FABRICS

When cutting out shapes to appliqué to a quilt, everyone reaches for fusible web. But if you use a lightweight web, you can use it for all aspects of your art quilt. You can make interfacing for delicate fabrics, baste a quilt without getting poked by sharp quilting pins, and even add subtle shading effects with delicate fabrics.

I use Mistyfuse, a particularly lightweight, solvent-free fusible web, for all of these techniques (and more). It stays soft and creates a strong bond. (If you use a different brand of fusible web, then your results may differ from mine.) Because I use fusible web in almost every step of making a quilt, I apply it to my fabrics before I embark on a new project.

Pre-fuse Fabric Pieces

I like to pre-fuse all of my fabrics so that when I'm ready to start creating, I can just grab the fabrics and start cutting without having to stop and add fusible web to a piece that I want to use. The most important thing to remember when fusing web to fabric is to never touch the surface of the iron to the web. It will melt onto the surface of the iron and make a mess.

> **FUSING TIP** *If you melt fusible web onto your iron plate (and trust me, it happens to everyone at least once!), run the hot iron over an unused dryer fabric softener sheet. This will help clean off the surface of the iron quickly.*

Place the fabric on your ironing surface wrong side up. Place a layer of fusible web on top of the fabric, cover it with either a piece of parchment paper or a Teflon pressing sheet, and press with a hot, dry iron (no steam). It's important to iron the entire area thoroughly; otherwise, the fusible web will pull away from the fabric.

Allow the surface to cool for a moment, and then peel back the parchment paper or remove the pressing sheet. Set the fused

parchment paper tracing

figure 1: Do not reverse your shapes when tracing them.

figure 2: Use a hot iron to transfer your design from parchment paper to fabric.

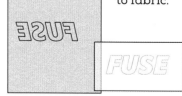

figure 3: Cut the design out from the back of the fabric.

MAKING MISTYFUSE NO-REVERSE APPLIQUÉS

Step 1: Trace your design into parchment paper with a pencil.

Step 2: Place fabric on the tracing, Mistyfuse side down, and iron to transfer the design.

Step 3: Cut out the design and fuse it to your quilt.

MAKING TRANSFER PAPER NO-REVERSE APPLIQUÉS

Step 1: Trace over the design to transfer the chalk to the back of the fabric.

Step 2: Reveal the chalk design transferred to the back of the fabric.

fabric aside to cool completely; then you can fold the fabric up and store it just as you would any other fabric. If the fused fabric is still warm, the fused surface will stick to itself.

If the stored, folded fabric wrinkles, just press the wrinkles out with a piece of parchment paper or Teflon pressing sheet against the fused side.

> **FUSING TIP** *If you are using baking parchment as your pressing sheet, clip a small piece off the lower right hand corner and, whenever you use it, make sure that the clipped corner is always in the lower right hand corner. This ensures that the same side will always be against the fusible web.*

No-reverse Appliqués

If you've experimented with appliqué, you might remember the chore of having to reverse your pattern shapes before cutting them out of fabric, else they end up backward. This can be especially tedious and confusing when working with text. But with my work forward technique, you'll eliminate the need to have to reverse your designs.

Begin by tracing your design onto a piece of parchment paper using a pencil - do not reverse the design **(figure 1)**. If you are going to cut your design out of a dark piece of fabric, use a white- or yellow-colored pencil.

Fuse a layer of Mistyfuse to the wrong side of your fabric. Place the fabric on top of the parchment paper, taking care to lay the fusible web side down against the parchment paper. Iron with a hot iron on a firm surface **(figure 2)**.

When you peel the fabric off the parchment paper, you'll see that the design you traced onto the parchment paper has been transferred to the back of the fabric. Now you can cut your pattern piece out of the fabric along the transferred line and fuse it to your quilt **(figure 3)**.

Some materials in your art quilt might not react well to heat, but you want to add an appliqué anyway. When you can't use fusible web, you can use a transfer paper technique instead to transfer your design to the backside of your fabric without having to reverse it.

Step 1: Fuse crinkled fabric to muslin.

Step 2: Baste fabric.

Step 3: Paint the top layer.

Step 4: Press and paint again.

Several different brands of transfer paper are on the market, including graphite-based and wax-based products. But my favorite type is a chalk-based transfer paper called Transdoodle. Unlike wax or graphite, the chalk cannot be made permanent by heat and easily brushes off the surface of fabric.

To use Transdoodle to transfer your appliqué design to fabric, place the paper on your work surface with the chalk side up. Put your fabric on top with the wrong side against the transfer paper. Place your design on top of the fabric, and then use a blunt pencil to trace your design (page 25). The chalk from the paper will transfer to the wrong side of your fabric.

Add Unique Texture

I developed this technique while searching for a way to make a permanently textured silk surface that I could paint. You can use this technique with colored or printed fabric. My favorite way to use it is with white fabrics that I then add layers of paint to. The resulting fabric is a one-of-a-kind surface rich with texture, dimension, and color.

To create a textured surface, you'll need two fabrics: the top layer that you'll steam and wrinkle, plus the bottom layer that you'll fuse the top layer to. The top layer can be anything you want—I like to use a very lightweight silk Habotai (5mm). An inexpensive muslin with two layers of fusible web already applied works best for the bottom layer.

This is one of the few times in my studio when I use a steam iron; if you don't have one, you can do this technique by misting the silk lightly before you crumple it.

Crumple your top layer fabric up into a ball and then crush it with an iron set to steam. While pressing the iron onto the crumpled ball of silk, press the steam button on the iron. Set the iron aside, open the fabric, and then crumple it up again. Steam press the crumpled ball again. Depending on the fabric that you're working with, you may have to repeat this process several times to get the amount of wrinkling that you want.

Next, lay your muslin with the fusible web side up on your ironing surface. Open up the crumpled, wrinkled fabric and lay it on top of the muslin. Spread the wrinkled fabric out loosely on the muslin. Use a very hot iron to press the wrinkled surface onto the muslin, using an up and down pressing motion. Fusing the wrinkled layer to the muslin layer preserves all of the interesting, textured lines made by the wrinkles.

After I've completed pressing and fusing the wrinkled top layer, I turn the piece over and iron the entire surface from the back.

Press the entire surface, then run a basting stitch around the edges with your sewing machine before you paint the fabric.

Paint the surface of the top layer. You may find that the moisture from the paint loosens the fused bond of the fabrics. Once the paint is dry, just re-press the surface with a hot iron using a piece of muslin or parchment paper as a press cloth. Add many different layers of paint, and after each layer dries, press the surface before adding more paint. After adding many layers of paint, you may need to use steam to get a good press once the piece is finished.

Shade with Fabrics

The more you heat Mistyfuse, the more translucent it becomes, so it's possible to use it with delicate, sheer fabrics such as polyester organza and toile if you are careful. After you add the Mistyfuse to a piece of sheer fabric, you can fuse it to your quilt to create shadowing or to tone down a too-bright fabric.

The fusible web will still be on the surface of the cloth, but with enough heat, you won't really see it, as long as you use parchment paper as your press cloth. If you use a Teflon pressing sheet, then you'll notice that the surface has a shine to it.

Use lightweight fusible web to create one-of-a-kind shades of solid fabrics.

Create Unique Interfacing

If the fabric that you want to use for your project is too lightweight or too sheer, you can create interfacing to stabilize it. Simply fuse a layer of Mistyfuse to a piece of plain white or neutral lightweight cotton, silk, or other material that, in turn, can be fused to the backside of the fabric you want to stabilize.

I often apply this technique when I'm working with a light-colored fabric, such as yellow or peach, that will be fused on top of a darker color. The lighter colored fabric becomes more opaque and obscures the darker color beneath it.

Baste Quilt Layers

Basting your quilt layers together with Mistyfuse avoids the use of pins, making it easier to quilt. Keep a basket or shoebox near your pressing station and toss in the bits of fusible web you've trimmed off of your fabric pieces. Fuse them in random spots on your quilt top and backing. You can then fuse both of them to the batting. If you have no bits and scraps on hand, just cut or tear strips of fusible web to use.

Coloring with Metallics

You can also easily add textile foil or metal leaf to the surface of your quilt using a lightweight fusible web. Textile foil comes in a variety of colors, which you can buy by the sheet or yard. Unlike metal leaf, textile foil doesn't require a delicate touch to use and tends to be less expensive. Whichever one you use is a matter of personal preference.

Textile foil is a layer of foil attached to a clear film. When the foil is bonded to a surface, the clear film is lifted away and the foil remains on the surface. It's usually marketed with a liquid adhesive, but I prefer, instead, to use Mistyfuse to bond it to the surface of fabric projects.

Deborah Boschert

As I think back on the places I have called home, it's amazing to remember the different views outside the windows. My personal view has also changed as we've moved from state to state.

For this small art quilt, I thought it would be fun to shift the windows to suggest a changing view. I used pre-fused organza and chiffon for the windows and experimented with placement to create different layers of design.

The landscape elements in this composition not only allow me to play with different fabrics and surface designs, but also suggest the adventure of exploring different places and ideas. I stamped those green circles with acrylic paint and a jar to look like clouds in a yellow sky.

I especially love hand embroidery. There are tiny French knots like buds on the wispy tree and green stitches that could be wild flowers stretching right across the house and onto the hillside.

Free-form fused appliqué gives me freedom to cut any shape. That's part of the allure of creating art quilts and exploring stitching and fabric.

Windows Arise
12" × 12"
(30.5 × 30.5 cm)

FOILING TIP *Textile foil can be confusing to use because the natural inclination is to assume that the colored side is the actual foil. However, there is a clear film on the colored side that you can't see until you've removed some of the foil beneath. So, whenever you use textile foil with fusible web, the fusible should always be against the noncolored side of the foil.*

Textile foil: I use two methods to adhere textile foil to fabric with Mistyfuse.

One way is to tear or cut small pieces of Mistyfuse, then iron them to the fabric using parchment paper as the press cloth. Next, place the textile foil, colored side up, on top of the fusible web. Cover it with a piece of parchment paper. Press the foil in place with a hot iron. Do not sweep the iron back and forth over the surface, as this may result in unwanted wrinkles.

You don't want the iron to sit on the surface in one spot for too long, and you may have to experiment with how long to iron the surface to get the best results. Let the surface cool completely before you peel back the foil.

For the second method, add a layer of Mistyfuse to the back of the textile foil first.

Place a piece of fusible web on top of a piece of parchment paper, then place the textile foil, colored side up, on top of the parchment paper. Cover with another piece of parchment paper, then iron to bond the fusible web to the foil. Remove the top layer of parchment paper, but do not peel the textile foil off of the bottom piece of parchment paper. Leaving the foil attached to the parchment paper makes it easier to handle the foil and cut out shapes from it. If you have a die cutter, you can run the foil and parchment paper through it to cut shapes.

After you've cut out the shape, remove the parchment paper and place the foil on the fabric. Cover it with a new piece of parchment paper and press it with a hot iron. Leave it to cool completely. Carefully peel back the clear film attached to the foil. It can be helpful to use a sharp pin to gently pry back a bit of the film, which you can then grab with a pair of tweezers.

Metal leaf: Metal leaf can be trickier to work with than textile foil because it's so thin. The slightest breeze or movement will cause it to move off the backing paper, so you definitely don't want to work in front of an open window or fan.

Put a piece of parchment paper on your ironing surface. Very carefully slide a piece of the metal leaf out of the package and onto the parchment paper. Place a piece of Mistyfuse over the top of the metal leaf, cover with a piece of parchment paper, and then press with a hot iron. Let it cool before lifting up the parchment paper with the attached metal leaf.

Now you can either cut out your shapes—it's easier to do this if you leave the parchment paper attached—or you can very carefully pull the metal leaf off the parchment paper and then fuse it to your project.

Alternatively, you can fuse the web to the fabric before you add the metal leaf. After applying Mistyfuse to your fabric, cover it with metal leaf, then press with a hot iron, using parchment paper as a press cloth. Let the surface cool for a moment and then brush off any excess metal leaf with a stiff brush.

Care must be taken when laundering any project that has textile foil or metal leaf on it. Hand washing is recommended. Do not put any foiled surfaces through the dryer. When ironing a foiled surface, always use a parchment paper press cloth or a Teflon sheet.

Painting Fusible Web

The only time Mistyfuse gets sticky is when you apply heat to it. When it's not heated, it acts like any other thin, gossamer-like fabric. You can get some interesting effects when you paint fusible web and then adhere it to the surface of fabric. You can use any acrylic paint on Mistyfuse—metallic paints yield particularly stunning results.

Wearing rubber gloves, tear off a piece of fusible web and dab it into a small amount of paint. Knead the color through the Mistyfuse until it's distributed evenly. Depending on how much paint you picked up and how big a piece you are working with, you may have to add a bit more.

You can hang it to dry or leave it to dry flat on a piece of parchment paper. Once the paint is dry, you can fuse it to the top of your fabric as a decorative element. It just becomes a part of the surface, and it doesn't need to have any other fabric fused on top of it. Or you can use it in place of plain Mistyfuse when applying foil to your fabric or to add a subtle layer of color underneath a sheer fabric.

ARTIST SPOTLIGHT

Lyric Kinard

Cephalopods of the subclass Ammonoidea capture my imagination with their beautiful spirals of Fibonacci perfection. Rather than trying to recreate a realistic record of an ammonite, I have used painted and foiled Mistyfuse to hint at the rich combination of time and materials that have created one of nature's beautiful works of art.

My process is to place Mistyfuse onto crumpled then smoothed parchment paper. Watered-down textile paints are applied and allowed to dry. The crinkles in the paper allow water and paint to pool in interesting textures. Once dry, the Mistyfuse is layered with another piece of parchment or a Teflon pressing sheet, flattened, and fused to the parchment. It is then cut or torn into shapes and applied to the surface of the cloth. After the paper is removed, a fresh sheet of parchment is placed over the exposed fusible so that an iron can be heated enough to adhere a sheet of foil gently rubbed on while it is still hot.

A solid sheet of Mistyfuse is adhered to the back of the batting before the backing cloth is laid on top of the quilt, sewn around all four sides, slit, trimmed, then turned right side out. Starting at the edges, the backing material is carefully positioned and ironed down towards the slit. A label is simply fused over the top of the slit that was used to turn the piece.

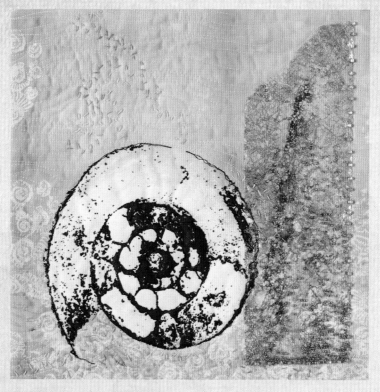

Ammonite VIII
12" × 12" (30.5 × 30.5 cm)

CHAPTER four
quilt it!

One of the hardest and most overwhelming decisions to make when creating an art quilt can be how to quilt it. Instead of agonizing over a complex quilting design, let the quilting play a supporting role. Keep it simple and allow the colors and imagery of your art quilt to be the stars.

Quilting Considerations
FOR THE BEGINNING ART QUILTER

For the beginning art quilter, deciding how to quilt your designs can be the most challenging part of making a quilt. My motto when it comes to quilting is "keep it simple." When I create an art quilt, I want the imagery and colors to be the first thing that the viewer notices. The imagery draws the viewer in, and the quilting and embellishments become supporting elements that should enhance but not overpower or detract from the imagery.

I always choose a thread color that is close to the color of the fabric that I'm quilting. I use the same color in the bobbin. I usually work with cotton thread, but sometimes a shiny polyester or shimmering metallic thread can add a nice element of surprise to a quilt.

When it comes to the actual quilting, you can either free-motion quilt your piece or straight stitch it. My quilts usually have a combination of both. I use free-motion stitching to fill in larger background areas, and then I use straight stitching to quilt individual elements, letting the shape of each element dictate the design that I use.

QUILTING TIP *As with any skill, free-motion quilting takes practice. Make a few 12" × 12" (30.5 × 30.5 cm) quilt sandwiches using scrap fabric and batting and keep them next to your sewing machine. Take five or ten minutes a day to practice stitching on the sandwiches. You may need to play with stitch length and tension settings, which vary depending on the fabrics and the number of layers that have been applied to the base fabric. Practice will make you more comfortable and confident when stitching on your art pieces.*

Free-Motion Quilting

When setting up your sewing machine for free-motion quilting, make sure that your bobbin is full and that you have the appropriate needle installed. You'll need to drop your sewing machine's feed dogs and install a free-motion or open toe foot (consult your sewing machine's user manual for instructions).

If you are working on a large quilt, you may find it helpful to roll up the sides of the quilt that you are not stitching. This will prevent them from draping over the edge of your sewing surface and distorting your stitches.

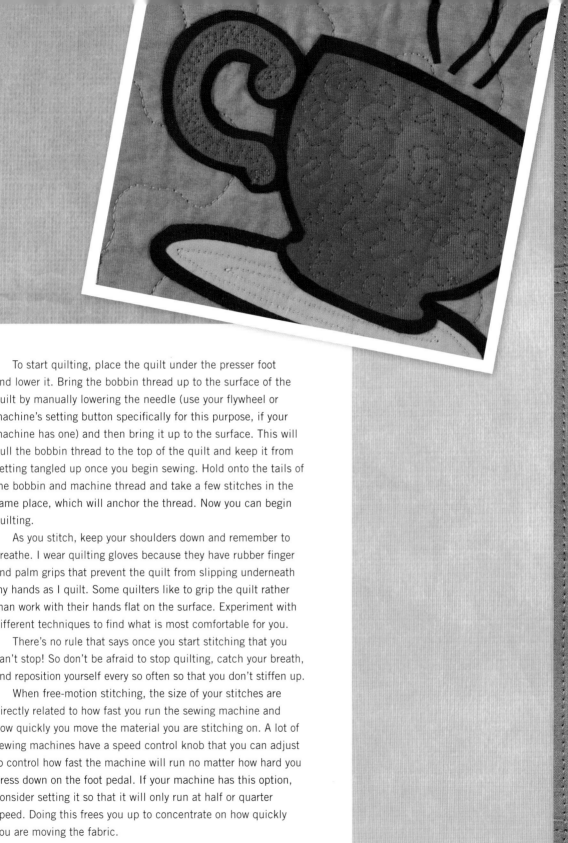

To start quilting, place the quilt under the presser foot and lower it. Bring the bobbin thread up to the surface of the quilt by manually lowering the needle (use your flywheel or machine's setting button specifically for this purpose, if your machine has one) and then bring it up to the surface. This will pull the bobbin thread to the top of the quilt and keep it from getting tangled up once you begin sewing. Hold onto the tails of the bobbin and machine thread and take a few stitches in the same place, which will anchor the thread. Now you can begin quilting.

As you stitch, keep your shoulders down and remember to breathe. I wear quilting gloves because they have rubber finger and palm grips that prevent the quilt from slipping underneath my hands as I quilt. Some quilters like to grip the quilt rather than work with their hands flat on the surface. Experiment with different techniques to find what is most comfortable for you.

There's no rule that says once you start stitching that you can't stop! So don't be afraid to stop quilting, catch your breath, and reposition yourself every so often so that you don't stiffen up.

When free-motion stitching, the size of your stitches are directly related to how fast you run the sewing machine and how quickly you move the material you are stitching on. A lot of sewing machines have a speed control knob that you can adjust to control how fast the machine will run no matter how hard you press down on the foot pedal. If your machine has this option, consider setting it so that it will only run at half or quarter speed. Doing this frees you up to concentrate on how quickly you are moving the fabric.

Marking Quilting Designs

Sometimes you may find it helpful to mark quilting lines on your quilt, which act as a guide as you stitch. Many different marking tools are available. The one you choose will depend on the method you can use to remove the marks from your art quilt.

Water-soluble pens work great, but you will have to expose your quilt to water to wash out the marked lines. This may not be feasible for wall quilts that you've created with mixed-media techniques involving paper or other nontraditional materials.

Disappearing ink pens are filled with an ink that fades over time when exposed to air. Of course, you must stitch quickly before the lines fade away. Most chalk-based pencils or tailor's chalk will rub off the surface of your quilt over time. Mechanical pencils made for marking on fabric make a very fine line but are only removable with an eraser. They're good for marking lines that you will stitch over using a dark thread.

My choice for marking is iron-off chalk. This is a specially formulated chalk that completely disappears from the surface of the fabric when it's ironed. Because it comes in a bottle, you have to decant it into another container to use it for marking. I purchased a chalk wheel, emptied out the chalk that it came with, and refilled it with the iron-off chalk.

Jamie Fingal

My mantra for creating art is to "work original, have fun, and love what I do." These ideas frame the trailer, flowers, and bunting flags in this quilt. My inspiration? Let's go on a road trip and discover something about ourselves.

When I get ready to do a project, I apply Mistyfuse to all of the fabrics, usually one-half yard to one yard (45.5 cm to 1 meter) at a time. As you can imagine, I have plenty of leftovers for another project. I can take all of those scraps and make a quilt that looks like a panel but really isn't.

The sky and landscape of "work original" are made totally out of scraps from my own line of fabric called "Home Is Where Your Story Begins." The prints include the text, flowers, house, and blue circles I used to create this piece. I easily made new words—"sew," "fun," and "art"—too. Gotta love that!

My pieces are made on a wool-blend felt foundation. I make my piece, iron the entire panel onto the wool-blend felt, and trim the edges. The piece is backed with another piece of wool-blend felt, usually some fun color such as hot pink or fire engine red, and then free-motion machine quilted.

work original
12" x 12" (30.5 x 30.5 cm)

Basic Free-Motion Designs

The thought of free-motion stitching can be daunting, especially for beginning quilters. But it's really not hard to do! Start with easy, basic styles, such as meandering, swirls, and nested boxes. These are not only easy to master but they also make great background cover for large areas and add wonderful visual texture for small areas of your quilts.

Meandering: The easiest background design to quilt is a random meandering pattern **(figure 1)**. I use it a lot. I usually start in the center of the quilt and work my way out toward the edges. As I stitch, I am careful not to sew over any previously stitched lines. If I am quilting a large quilt, then I don't stitch the area too densely. For smaller pieces, I use a more densely stitched design.

Swirls: Swirls are also an easy pattern to stitch **(figure 2)**. I like to use them for the sky in my art quilts. The only caveat to stitching swirls is that you have to remember to give yourself enough room to stitch out of the center of the design. You'll be sewing in concentric circles from the outside to the inside, and when you reverse your way back to the outside of the circle, you'll need to have enough room for your stitches. Keep that in mind while you're sewing, and don't stitch your lines too close together.

figure 1 - Meandering

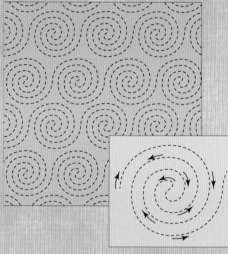

figure 2 - Swirls

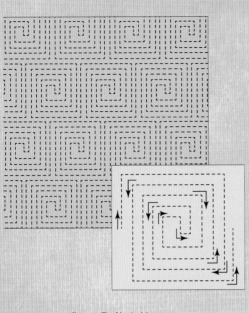

figure 3 - Nested boxes

Nested boxes: Nested boxes are stitched the same way as swirls, but you work with straight lines instead of curved ones **(figure 3)**. You have to give yourself enough room to stitch out of the center of the box toward the outside edge of the quilt, so remember not to stitch your lines too closely together.

Straight-Stitch Quilting Ideas

If you're not interested in free-motion stitching, there's no rule that says you can't use straight stitching on your art quilt. Even with the feed dogs up and the presser foot engaged, your quilting can be artful and energetic.

Waves: This pattern also works nicely for quilting skies or oceans **(figure 4)**. Just start at one outside edge of your quilt, and, as you stitch across the surface, slowly move the quilt left and right to create a gently curved wavy pattern. When you reach the opposite outside edge, cut the thread. Repeat to add more rows until your background is filled.

figure 4 - Waves

Follow the edge: Let the shape of the image you're quilting guide your stitching line when you're quilting individual motifs **(figure 5)**. If I'm stitching the roof of a house, I will start at one corner and follow the shape of the roof until I reach the center, creating a sort of angled spiral. You can do this inside of any shape. It can get a little tricky when following the edge of a curved element, but if you take your time and stitch slowly, you'll get great results.

Grids: Grids are really easy to stitch and they make great filler patterns for both large and small areas **(figure 6)**. Use your favorite marking tool to draw straight lines to stitch over or just draw the first and use the edge of the presser foot for each subsequent line. There's also no rule that says your grid has to be made up of just straight lines. Try stitching wavy lines instead of straight ones or use zigzag stitches to add even more visual interest.

Post-Quilting Tips

When you're done quilting the surface of your quilt, you're left with those pesky thread tails from bringing the bobbin thread up to the surface. You can either cut them off very close to the top of the quilt or use a sewing needle to pull them to the back of the work.

After I've finished quilting, I always press my quilts (using a pressing cloth if I'm ironing a painted surface) to iron out any wrinkles that may have formed while manipulating the quilt during the quilting process. Once it's pressed, I tack it up on my design wall, take a few steps back, and start thinking about any embellishments I want to add.

figure 5 - Follow the edge

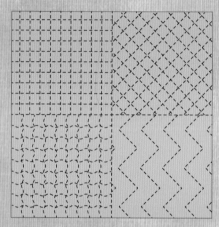

figure 6 - Grids

Leslie Tucker Jenison

Labels have a dual meaning. They are a way to identify a brand and provide information. They are also used in a negative social context to create boundaries between groups. Generic brands versus recognizable (desirable) clothing are a frequent social barrier in middle school and beyond.

I'm interested in the information contained in each label as well as the artistry of each one. We assign meaning to them. They become status symbols of quality and current fashion.

Socially, labels can be harmful: the "slow reader" in school, the "nerd," the "misfit." Once given, labels are difficult to overcome in a cultural context.

The materials used in this piece include clothing labels, hand-dyed silk organza, Mistyfuse, commercially-printed cotton, felt, and cotton and polyester thread. I used several techniques to create this piece, including fusing, die-cutting fabric, machine stitching, and free-motion quilting. Labels were fused to commercial cotton and stitched into place. Silk organza was fused, die-cut twice, and then fused to the label surface. It was free-motion quilted.

Labels
12" × 12" (30.5 × 30.5 cm)

CHAPTER five

embellish it!

Adding embellishments such as hand-stitched embroidery, funky buttons, glittery beads, shimmery sequins, or deftly hand-painted details to a quilt can provide a special finishing touch. It's also a creative way to highlight a focal point of your imagery that deserves a closer look.

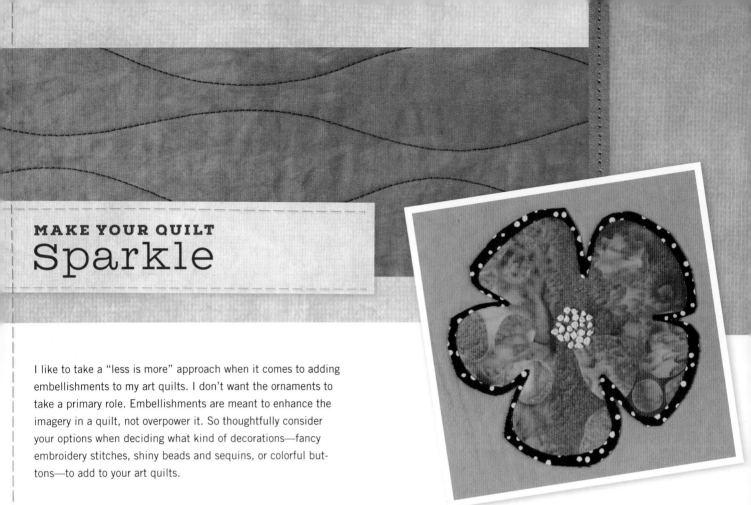

MAKE YOUR QUILT
Sparkle

I like to take a "less is more" approach when it comes to adding embellishments to my art quilts. I don't want the ornaments to take a primary role. Embellishments are meant to enhance the imagery in a quilt, not overpower it. So thoughtfully consider your options when deciding what kind of decorations—fancy embroidery stitches, shiny beads and sequins, or colorful buttons—to add to your art quilts.

Stitching by Hand

Hand stitching is an easy way to add a bit of texture, detail, and color to your quilts. It also allows you to work with yarns and threads that are too thick to use in your sewing machine. You can hand stitch with any thread as long as the needle has an eye large enough to accommodate the thickness of the thread and it pierces the fabric with a large enough hole to allow the thread to pass through it.

You can use any of hundreds of embroidery stitches to add hand-stitched details to your quilts. Whole books have been written on the subject! These are a few of my favorite embroidery stitches.

French knot: French knots are an easy way to add texture to your quilts. They work beautifully in the center of flowers, for example, or as doorknobs in place of buttons. French knots make wonderful filler for areas where you want to add a spot of color and texture.

To tie a French knot, first bring your thread up through your fabric from the wrong side to the right side **(figure 1)**. Wrap the thread around the needle two or three times. While holding the thread tautly with your other hand, insert the needle close to where you came up through the fabric from the wrong side of the fabric. Finally, pull the thread through to the wrong side to tighten the knot on the surface.

Couching: For threads too thick to pass through the eye of a needle, you can couch threads to tack them to your quilt. Consider couching for the stem of a flower or several yarns couched in a grouping to imitate tree bark. When used to outline a shape on your quilt with a different color thread, couching adds bold dimensional accents to the imagery.

Couching can be done by hand or machine, depending on the thickness of the thread. To couch by hand, place the heavier thread (known as the laid, couching, or working thread) you want to tack down on your quilt top, and then hold the heavy thread in place with one hand and hand stitch over it with a matching or contrasting color thread **(figure 2)**. Begin stitching at one end of the couching thread and finish at the opposite end. Keep your

figure 1 - French knot

figure 2 - Couching

figure 3 - Split stitch

stitches close to the sides of the thick thread you are couching in place. You can work from right to left or left to right.

To couch by machine, set your sewing machine on a zigzag stitch wide enough to pass over the couching thread. You want the needle to land just to the left and just to the right of the thread. It's a good idea to practice before stitching on your art quilt.

Split stitch: A split stitch works well as an outline stitch for any element on your art quilts. I like to use it to add the vein details on leaves. Embroidery floss, perle cotton, and tapestry or crewel thread work well for this stitch.

To make a row of split stitches, working from left to right, bring your needle up through your fabric from the wrong side to the right side and then take a small stitch (⅛ to ¼ inches [3 mm to 6 mm] long) back down to the wrong side of the fabric. Bring the needle back up to the right side through the center of the stitch you just made, between the strands of the thread **(figure 3)**. This splits the thread in half. Take another small stitch back down to the wrong side of the fabric.

When using this stitch to outline a curved image, keep your stitches short and of an even size to maintain a smooth curve.

Attaching Baubles

Stitch dimensional embellishments such as beads, sequins, buttons, or charms thoughtfully to your quilt; otherwise they could detract from the overall visual impact. Rather than beading an entire leaf, consider beading just the veins. Too many buttons may overpower your quilt's imagery and look crafty. Use them as a way to add spots of dimensional details such as doorknobs, flower centers, or eyes. Keep in mind that the weight of large, heavy beads or charms may distort your quilt, so use them with care and make sure to secure them in place with a sturdy thread.

Barb Forrister

"Mystique" is a three-dimensional soft-sculpted floral arrangement made with an array of mixed media techniques. The background was hand dyed with fiber-reactive dyes, silk-screened, stamped, and stenciled with acrylic paints.

The large irises consist of painted muslin and crinoline that have been fused together and stitched. Crinoline is essentially a wire mesh fabric that is often used to make hats, so it is wonderful for sculpting shapes. The stems are tubes of fabric with drinking straws inserted, which offers an alternative round yet malleable shape.

Other flowers include one large pink and yellow blossom made from painted and heat-distressed Lutradur, as well as two smaller flowers that have been embellished with beads and cording. The leaves were created by fusing bits of leftover thread, fibers, and scraps of hand-dyed lace to upholstery and cotton fabrics to impart texture and provide a tactile organic essence to the foliage.

I have created several three-dimensional soft-sculpted pieces in this manner. My preferred fusible web is Mistyfuse because it is lightweight, does not gum up the needles when stitching, and has tiny fingerlike projections that grab the fibers and allow the layers to become integrated with each other. This is especially important when designing sculpted quilts with thick texture.

Mystique
12" × 12" (30.5 × 30.5 cm)

Buttons: I love to use buttons as detail elements in my quilts. For the projects in this book, I've used them for doorknobs and placed them in the center of flowers.

To sew buttons onto your quilts, use a couple of strands of embroidery floss and dab the knot with a bit of seam sealer. If you tie the knot on the top of the button, then you get the added texture from the thread tails, which looks particularly artful when you've used the button as the center of a flower.

Beads and sequins: Adding beads to a quilt can be a great way to add shimmer and sparkle as well as color, texture, and dimension. When used thoughtfully, the right amount of beading can catch the viewer's eye from a distance.

It's important to use a good quality thread for beading. You don't want to spend a lot of time adding beads to your quilt and then have them fall off because the thread isn't strong enough to hold them in place or shreds when it comes into contact with the bead. Beads with sharp edges, including crystals, bugle beads, and shells, require the use of a tough beading thread. Fireline beading thread is made of very strong gel-spun polyethylene that resists shredding.

When working with smooth-edged seed beads, you have several more choices for beading thread. Nymo, Superion, and Silamide are some of the brands available, and each comes in a range of colors.

The only requirement for a needle is that the eye is small enough to pass through the bead and strong enough to pierce your quilted fabrics.

I always use a single strand of thread rather than doubling it, unless I am adding a large, heavy bead. As a general rule, I use a thread color that matches the dominant color of the beads. If I'm using a combination of bead colors, then I use a thread that matches the color of the fabric.

To sew a seed bead onto your quilt, start with a length of thread measuring 12 to 18 inches (30.5 to 45.5 cm) long and knot one end. Bring the needle up to the right side from the wrong side, put a bead on your needle, and push the bead down the length of thread to the quilt top. Insert your needle back into the fabric and pull the thread to the wrong side.

For added security, you can sew back through the bead again and then back into the quilt on the other side of the bead before continuing to add more beads to the surface of your quilt. The extra stitch is particularly helpful when working with large or heavy beads.

If you'd like to add a sequin underneath your seed bead, thread a sequin onto your needle, pick up a seed bead, and insert your needle back through the hole in the sequin and through the quilt to the wrong side. Repeat to add more sequins and beads. The beads help hold the sequin in place.

> **BEADING TIP** *Stop and add a knot to the back of your work after sewing four or five beads to your quilt before continuing to sew on more beads. If your thread breaks while you are sewing, you will lose only the beads that you've added since the most recent knot that you tied.*

To add a line of seed beads to your quilt, bring your needle up through your quilt from the wrong side, pick up four beads, and push them down the length of thread to the surface of the quilt top. Insert your needle back into the quilt and pull the thread to the wrong side. Sew back through to the top of the quilt, bringing the needle up in the space between the second and third bead, and then reinsert the needle through the holes of the third and fourth bead. Pick up four more beads and continue sewing them on in this manner until you've added all the beads you want.

Decorating with Paint and Colored Pencils

You can also use paint to embellish your art quilt. Perhaps you want a particular area of your quilt to stand out, or maybe you want to add some shading to the underside of a leaf or make the center of a flower brighter and bolder. Because your quilt will not be washed, you can use any acrylic paint to add a spot of color anywhere.

Be sure to test your paint on a scrap of fabric first before you attempt to paint on your quilt. You can see if the paint bleeds or spreads beyond the area you apply it to. In general, the thinner the paint, the more it will bleed.

Alternatively, you could use colored pencils instead of paint. Using a colored pencil will give you more control over the placement of the color. Derwent Inktense pencils are available in strong, vibrant colors and can be used wet or dry. Color them onto a dry fabric and then use a water-wetted paintbrush or a water-filled barrel paintbrush to blend them to create a more translucent effect.

Terri Stegmiller

During the spring and summer months, I spend lots of time in my flower garden. Growing and tending colorful flowers is so relaxing, and digging around in the dirt and pulling weeds offers plenty of opportunity for inspiration. Over the years I have done many things to lure more birds to my yard. I find it pleasurable to watch them come to eat and drink in my little paradise. Flowers and birds both make me happy, so they tend to show up a lot in my art.

Over the last few years, I have developed a mixed-media process that I love, and I enjoy translating my sketches and drawings into art quilt form using this process. My quilts start as a single piece of white fabric to which I add layers of color, design, and stitching. I am addicted to adding lots of textural quilting, and I also love painting, both of which I incorporate into my process.

At one point, I discovered that the addition of fused shapes on my mixed-media whole-cloth quilts adds even more interest and another layer of design . Because I add color to the quilts with layers of textile paints, the fabrics I prefer to use for my fused shapes are commercial prints that are white or cream with printed designs. When these types of fabrics are fused onto my quilts and then painted, the visual complexity increases and draws you in for closer inspection.

Flower Gazing
12" × 12" (30.5 × 30.5 cm)

finish it!

Because art quilts are designed to hang on a wall, safe from the wear and tear of a blanket thrown on a sofa or tucked into a bed, you can back and bind your art quilts in suitably nontraditional ways. I like to finish my art quilts with a false back and a black binding, creating a sharp frame for the imagery within. Try painting the edges or running a zigzag stitch around the outside instead of using a bias-tape binding. Don't limit yourself to traditional finishing techniques!

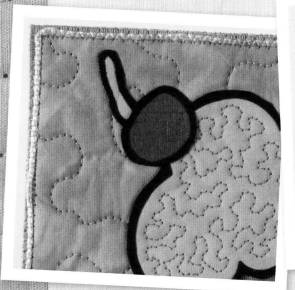

ADDING THE
Finishing Touches

You've fused a beautiful fabric collage of meaningful imagery, thoughtfully embellished it with just the right baubles, and carefully embroidered the focal point with hand stitching. Now, it's time to finish your art quilt. To add a backing and a binding to your art quilt, you can use similarly nontraditional techniques that will complement and harmonize with the finished quilt.

Backing Your Art Quilt

Even an art quilt requires a backing. I always use a false backing, which is simply a piece of fabric that's fused to the back of the quilt to hide all of the messy stitching. The fabric can coordinate with the quilt top, if you like, but it doesn't have to. In fact, I often buy a bolt of inexpensive fabric (inevitably, it's covered in an obnoxious print) to have on hand for false backs.

Cut a piece of fabric to the same size as the quilt top. Apply a layer of fusible web to the wrong side of it and then carefully fuse it to the back of the quilt. Then, trim the quilt to size and bind it.

Fusing the Binding

Each quilter has a favorite way to add a binding to a quilt, so if you already have a favorite binding, go ahead and use that. Nevertheless, my unconventional technique, the Four-Strip Binding Technique, is very easy. Unlike traditional methods to bind a quilt, my preferred way uses a separate binding strip for each side of the quilt. Each strip is stitched to the front of the quilt, then fused to the back, no tedious hand stitching required. I used this method to bind each art quilt project in this book.

THE FOUR-STRIP BINDING TECHNIQUE

2" (5 cm)

Step 1: Stitch the side strips.

Step 2: Fold, then press the strips.

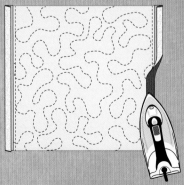

Step 3: Fuse the strips in place.

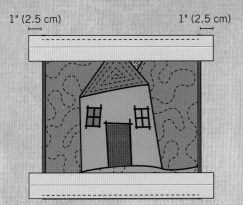

1" (2.5 cm) 1" (2.5 cm)

Step 4: Add the top and bottom strips.

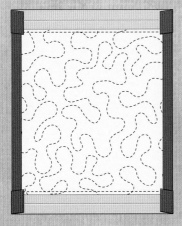

Step 5: Press the tail ends.

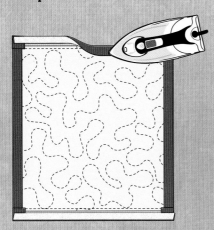

Step 6: Fuse the strips in place.

Step 7: Slip stitch the binding.

My Four-Strip Binding Technique

1. Measure the length (the side edges) of your quilt. Cut two 2" (5 cm) wide binding strips to that measurement. With the quilt top facing right side up, pin one binding strip on the left-hand edge of the quilt, with the right sides together. Align the raw edges, then stitch the binding strip in place using a ¼" (6 mm) seam allowance.

In the same manner, pin, then sew the second binding strip to the right-hand edge of the quilt.

2. Press the two binding strips flat. Turn the quilt over so that the backing faces up. Fold each of the binding strips in half lengthwise and press them to set the crease.

Cut two strips of fusible web 1" (2.5 cm) wide and as long as the binding strip. Fuse them in place lengthwise, aligning the fusible web strip with the raw edge of the binding strip. Let the fabric cool.

3. Fold the binding strip to the back of the quilt, making sure the creased edge of the binding strip fits snugly up next to the edge of the quilt. Use a hot iron to fuse it in place. Make sure the binding is fused securely so that it does not pull away from the back of the quilt.

4. Measure the top and bottom edges of your quilt and add 2" (5 cm) to each measurement. Cut two binding strips 2" (5 cm) wide and the width measurement of your quilt. Fold the two strips in half lengthwise and press to set the crease.

With the quilt top facing up, pin the strips in place to the top and bottom edges, right sides together, in the same manner as you applied the binding to the side edges of your quilt. Leave a 1" (2.5 cm) long tail extending past the edges of the quilt at each end. Stitch them in place using a ¼" (6 mm) seam allowance.

5. Press the binding strips flat. Turn the quilt over so that the quilt back faces up, then fold the tail ends over the edge and toward the back of the quilt. Press them again.

6. Repeat the same steps for folding, pressing, applying strips of fusible web, and fusing the binding strips in place as you did for the right and left-hand edges of the quilt.

7. If you plan to use your quilt as a throw or on your bed, you should make the bound edges more durable. Hand stitch the binding to secure it to the back of the quilt. Choose a thread color to match the binding and hand sew it in place using slip stitches. Keep your stitches as close to the edge of the binding as possible.

Unconventional Edges

Unlike traditional quilts, which must endure rigorous wear and tear on beds and couches, art quilts can be finished without a binding. There are many alternative ways to finish the edges of a wall quilt.

You could couch (page 44) a decorative trim or yarn around the outside edges. Use a zigzag stitch to attach decorative trims around the outside edges of your quilt. This will leave the edges of your quilt exposed, of course—an effect that you may like.

Try using a zigzag or satin stitch around the outside edges of your quilt to secure them. A variegated thread can provide an additional element of color and interest to your quilt.

You could even paint the outside edges with fabric paint. Use a foam brush and dab the edges of the quilt to secure them, similar to gluing the layers together. It may be helpful to run a line of straight stitching very close to the outside edge of the quilt first.

Another finish is similar to making a pillowcase. With right sides together, layer the backing fabric with the quilt top and sew around the edges, leaving a 6- to 8-inch-long (15 to 20.5 cm) opening for turning. Clip the corners to trim excess batting and fabric, then turn the quilt right side out through the opening. Press the quilt well, making sure that the backing doesn't show on the front of the quilt. If your quilt won't lie flat, stitch around the edges of the quilt on the front very close to the outside edge to prevent the backing from rolling toward the front. Then fold in the seam allowance toward the inside of the quilt, press, and fuse with a narrow strip of fusible web or slipstitch the opening closed.

My Four-Step Sleeve Method

Most art quilts are intended to hang on the wall, like any other piece of contemporary art. To turn your art quilt into a wall hanging, you'll need to add a sleeve to it so that you can run a dowel or slat through.

1. Measure the width of the quilt and subtract 1 inch (2.5 cm). Cut a piece of fabric 9" (23 cm) wide by the length that you calculated.

2. Hem each 9" (23 cm) side by folding the edge ½" (1.3 cm) toward the wrong side of the fabric and press with a hot iron. Fold again ½" (1.3 cm) to enclose the raw edge, press again, then sew along the folded edge of the fabric using a ¼" (6 mm) seam allowance.

3. Fold the fabric in half lengthwise with right sides together. Sew along the long raw edge using a ½" (1.3 cm) seam allowance to create a tube. Turn the tube right side out and press it so that the seam runs through the center of the tube. Crease the top and bottom long edges of the sleeve.

4. Lay the sleeve, with the seam flat against the back of the quilt, 1½" (3.8 cm) from the top edge. The seam won't be visible. Pin, then hand stitch the sleeve in place with slip stitches (page 53), beginning with the top creased edge. Finally, stitch the bottom long creased edge.

Kathy York

I have been thinking a lot about home lately as my children get older. When will they move away and leave me an empty nester? Will they know that they are welcome to come home at any time? I want both of my children to know that they are always welcome to live here at our home. Home conveys safety and love and family to me. Thus, the inspiration for this piece emerged, a theme of home with a tone of optimism that we can handle the changes that the future brings.

I selected a color palette that felt like spring, bright and light and colorful. The colors evoke a sense of hope and comfort. The fabrics were selected from both my stash of commercial cottons and fabrics that I created with batik and dye. I especially like the fabric choice for the sky because the colors fade from one color to another. It alludes to smooth transitions and evokes a sense of calm.

I created the composition like a collage. I fussy cut the batik flowers, each of which came from a different piece of fabric. I used a bit of fabric paint to create the chickadee's face. After the pieces were fused into place, I machine quilted it and added some hand stitching to both soften the hard edges and give it more texture. The edges were finished by wrapping the quilt around a stretched canvas.

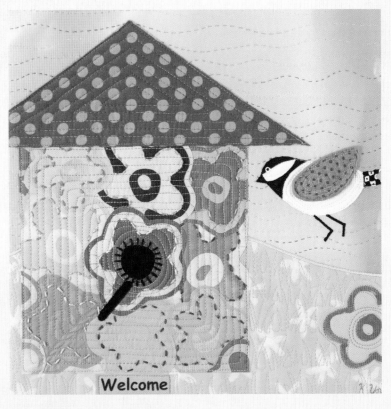

Welcome
12" × 12" (30.5 × 30.5 cm)

Mounting on Canvas

Mounting your art quilt on a stretched canvas can be a clever alternative to constructing a false backing, binding your quilt, and adding a hanging sleeve. A stretched canvas makes your quilt easy to hang, stabilizes it, and, depending on the depth of the canvas, makes for a sleek presentation as the quilt stands away from the wall.

If I plan to mount my quilt on a stretched canvas, I trim off any excess batting or wool felt that extends beyond the quilt top or the outside front edges of the canvas. This makes it easier to get a nice, neat corner when stretching the quilt onto the frame.

Place the finished quilt on top of the canvas. Wrap the edges of the quilt around to the back as neatly as you can, taking care to smooth the front of the quilt against the canvas.

I wrap the left- and right-hand edges first and then the top and bottom edges, stapling each in place with a staple gun. I like to trim off any extra fabric from the back and then cover the raw edge of the fabric with a piece of ribbon, securing it in place with fabric glue or hot glue.

Label Your Quilt

Lastly, you should always add a label to the back of your quilts. A label helps tell future generations—and collectors—the story of your quilt.

I print my labels out on inkjet-printable cotton sheets and then fuse or hand sew them onto the backs of my quilts. I always include this information on my labels:

- The name of the quilt
- The year it was completed
- The techniques I used
- Any statement relative to the quilt that I want to document
- My name and website address

If your quilt has been mounted on a stretched canvas, you can glue the label to the inside of the canvas or, if your canvas is deep enough, you can staple it to the inside edge of the canvas frame. If your quilt is a wall hanging, you can simply fuse it to the back.

"The Hummingbird"
2013
Hand Dyed Cotton, Machine Quilted

"Each spring I eagerly await the sight of the first hummingbird in the garden. This quilt celebrates the arrival of that exquisite moment"

Sue Bleiweiss
www.suebleiweiss.com

Desiree Habicht

Meet Wilson, my brother's French bulldog. He is one of my favorite subjects to paint, whether in pastels, watercolor, or fabric. Winston lives in Northern California near the coast, where the winters can be cold and foggy. When the sun starts to warm this beautiful part of the country, Winston is the first to be outside soaking up the rays. On this particular day, he was backlit, causing his ears to glow and a ring of white to surround him while the sun cast a strong shadow. I used fusible appliqué, paint, and pencils to create my little quilt of Winston sunbathing himself after a cold winter. Instead of binding this quilt, I used the pillowcase technique to finish the edges.

I love to create a glow in my work by using color and strong values. Being an artist, I love to combine the tactile element of fabric with paints and pencils to create a strong, eye-catching image.

When I am choosing my subject matter, strong lighting always inspires me. I also love a good story—each piece must say something to not only myself but to my viewers. Appliqué allows me to play not only with technique, but also with strong colors, often pushing outside of reality and into the surreal.

The Sunbather
12" × 12" (30.5 × 30.5 cm)

CHAPTER seven

create it!

Now, take your new fusing skills and make something amazing! Here are fourteen projects to get you started creating whimsical art quilts, vibrant table runners, and imaginative accessories. I designed these projects in my signature style—hand-dyed, candy-colored fabrics; stark black outlines; and a sprinkling of batik prints. You can replicate these projects as shown or use them as stepping stones to develop your own versions with the colors, fabrics, and imagery that you love most.

You'll use the same set of tools to make all of these fabric collage projects. In addition to the various fabrics, wool felt or batting, embellishments, and fusible web you'll choose for each one, have these tools close at hand:

- Tracing paper and a fine-point black marker for tracing the pattern drawings
- A chalk marker or other temporary marker for fabrics
- A rotary cutter, a self-healing mat, and a ruler
- A nonstick pressing sheet and an iron
- Thread that coordinates with your project fabrics

the
beach
house
ART QUILT

supplies

The Beach House drawing enlarged 225 percent

1 fat quarter of blue fabric for the background

1 fat quarter of brown fabric for the palm tree trunks

1 fat quarter of green fabric for the palm treetops

1 fat quarter of tan fabric for the sand

1 fat quarter of aqua fabric for the water

½ yd (45.5 cm) of black fabric for the outlines, house stilts, and binding

5 different fabric scraps, each 6" × 6" (15 × 15 cm), for the beach house

13" × 13" (33 × 33 cm) piece of muslin for the base

13" × 13" (33 × 33 cm) piece of wool felt for the batting

½ yd (45.5 cm) of coordinating fabric for the backing and hanging sleeve

1 package of Mistyfuse fusible web

A bead or button for the doorknob (optional)

FINISHED SIZE *12" × 12" (30.5 × 30.5 cm)*

The perfect size art quilt for a beginner is 12" × 12" (30.5 × 30.5 cm). It's not so big that it's overwhelming, and it's large enough for you to include a few fun details. However, don't let the small size fool you into thinking that it's a project for beginners only—the nine guest artists who created pieces for this book would surely disagree. The palette size may be limited, but room for your creativity isn't. Because they're small, you could make a series of Beach House quilts in different colorways or batiks and group them together on a wall for a splash of color.

The Beach House Drawing
Enlarge 225%

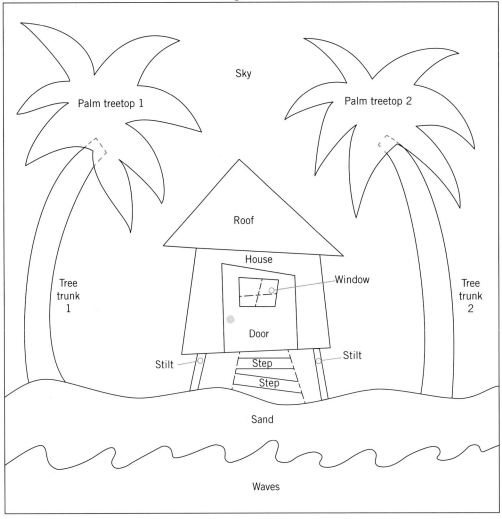

Prepare Pattern Pieces and Fabrics

1 Enlarge the drawing of the Beach House Art Quilt 225 percent so that it measures 12" × 12" (30.5 × 30.5 cm). You can use this as a template to make the quilt exactly as shown. Sketch your own elements on the enlarged drawing to customize the design.

2 Trace the drawing using tracing paper and a black marker. Cut the tracing apart on the marked lines to create your pattern pieces. Do not cut out the door's window, the steps, or the stilts. Those elements will be made later without patterns.

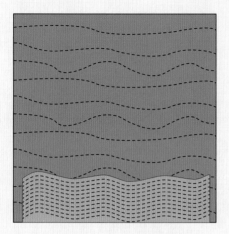

figure 1 - Quilt the sand.

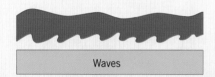

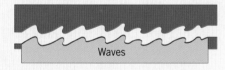

figure 2 - Outline the waves in black and trim to size.

3 Cut a 6" (15 cm) wide piece of black fabric along the width of the fabric. Reserve it for the binding.

Apply fusible web to the wrong side of all of your fabrics.

> **FUSING TIP** *When fusing fabrics onto the background of your quilt, make sure your iron is hot and you're using an up-and-down pressing motion rather than a side-to-side sweeping motion. Otherwise, you risk shifting the fusible web out of place. Once you've pressed the piece in place and it is secure, you can iron across the surface.*

Quilt the Background

4 Fuse the 13" × 13" (33 × 33 cm) piece of muslin to one side of the 13" × 13" (33 × 33 cm) piece of wool felt. Fuse the 13" × 13" (33 × 33 cm) square of blue fabric to the other side of the wool felt batting.

5 Quilt the blue background using your choice of quilting stitch.

I used straight stitches to create gently curved lines from one side edge to the other, spaced ¾" to 1" (2 to 2.5 cm) apart.

> **TROUBLESHOOTING TIP** *If your pieces don't bond well with the quilt and they pull away after the surface is cooled, your iron may not be hot enough. Make sure you're allowing enough time to press and applying enough pressure to the iron.*

Fuse the Sand and Waves

6 Using the pattern, cut out the sand piece from the tan fabric. Fuse it to the background, aligning the bottom straight edge of the sand piece with the bottom edge of the background.

7 Quilt the sand by following the top wavy edge as a guide for your quilting lines **(figure 1)**.

Again, I used straight stitches and made wavy lines, but spaced them only ¼" (6 mm) apart.

Making Cookie Cutter Outlines

I developed a technique to make what I call "cookie cutter" outlines. Similar to ripples in a pond, my cookie cutter outlines make it easy to create contrasting borders around organic shapes. Use this technique to make the black borders around the palm treetops in the Beach House quilt, as well as any image in any project that calls for radiating outlines.

First, cut out the shape from your tracing paper pattern.

Second, using a chalk marker, trace the shape on a piece of contrasting fabric that's at least ½" (6mm) larger on all sides than the shape. Cut it out from the contrasting fabric, starting at the center of the image.

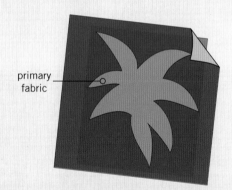

primary fabric

Third, discard the cut out shape. Fuse the piece of contrasting fabric on top of the piece of primary fabric, such as the green treetop piece.

Finally, trim the fused fabrics down to size, carefully following the lines of the cut out shape.

8 It's easier to outline the water's edge with a black strip of fabric before the waves piece is fused in place. This avoids having to work the black strip around the curvy edges. So, cut a 13" × 2" (33 × 5 cm) strip from the black fabric. Using the pattern piece for the water, cut the wavy edge along one long edge of the black fabric strip.

Cut a 13" × 2" (33 × 5 cm) strip from the aqua fabric. Place the black strip on top of the aqua strip, aligning the long straight edges. The wavy edge of the black strip will point toward the center of the aqua strip.

Fuse the black strip to the aqua strip. Trim the excess black fabric along the top wavy edge ⅛" to ¼" (3 to 6 mm) to make the outline **(figure 2, page 63)**. Set aside the remaining part of the black strip to use later.

Align the long straight edge of the water piece with the long straight edge of the sand and then fuse it in place.

9 Quilt the water by following the top wavy edge.

Add the Palm Trees

10 Using the pattern pieces, cut out the palm tree trunks and the palm treetops. Fuse them to the background, referring to the master pattern for placement.

11 Referring to "Making Cookie Cutter Outlines" on page 64, make a black outline for the treetops. Use a chalk marker to trace the treetop shape onto a square of black fabric larger than the treetop shape. Be sure to allow at least ½" (1.3 cm) around the outer edge of the traced shape. Cut the traced shape out of the fabric along the inner edges, leaving a ½" (1.3 cm) border around the outer edge.

12 Place the outline on top of your green fabric and fuse it in place. Trim the outer edge of the black outline to ¼" (6 mm) to complete the treetop.

Fuse the treetop to the quilt at the top of the tree trunk.

13 Quilt the palm tree trunks and tops, using their shapes as inspiration for your stitching pattern.

Creating Four-Step Windows

Many of my quilts feature buildings because I like how they can morph into wonky shapes. My skyscrapers, houses, and cabins all have windowpanes. This is a simple, four-step process for adding wonky windows to all of your buildings, from a simple beach house to a towering city office building.

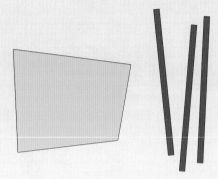

First, cut a wonky square or rectangle from your fabric. Place it on your ironing surface right side up. Cut several strips of fabric to use for your window panes and place them right side up.

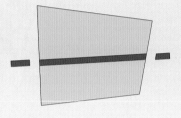

Second, fuse one black strip on the window shape horizontally. For a wonky look, skew the strip slightly. Trim to fit the width of the window.

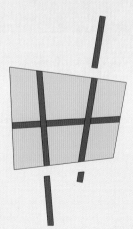

Third, fuse two strips on the windowpane vertically, skewing them a bit, too. Trim them to fit the length of the window.

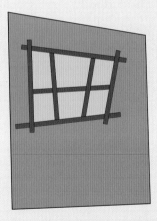

Finally, fuse the complete window to your building. Outline the window last with black or a different contrasting fabric to create a window frame. You can trim the outlines to exactly match the outside edge of the window or extend them a bit beyond the outside edge of the window to add more wonkiness to the design.

Build the Beach House

14 Use the pattern pieces to cut out the beach house and roof. Fuse them in place on the background, referring to the master pattern for placement.

15 Quilt the house and the roof sections separately using a straight stitch to echo the shape of each piece.

16 Use the pattern piece to cut out the door. Fuse it in place on the beach house.

17 Quilt the door using a straight stitch following the shape of the piece.

18 Make the window for the beach house door. Cut a wonky square shape for the window and place it on your ironing surface right side up. Cut six strips of black fabric ⅛" to ¼" (3 to 6 mm) wide by 1½" (3.8 cm) long for the windowpane and window outlines. (See "Creating Four-Step Windows.")

19 Place the black strips horizontally and vertically to create the window panes, trim them to the desired length, and fuse them in place.

20 Fuse the window onto the door, and then fuse black strips around the outside edges of the window to create a window frame.

I like to extend my outline strips beyond the edge of the windows, but you could trim them flush if you prefer.

21 To make the beach house stairs, cut two pieces of brown fabric 2" × ¼" (5 cm × 6 mm) and fuse them in place on the quilt. You may need to adjust the size of the stairs you cut to make them proportional to your version of the quilt.

22 Cut one black strip ⅛" to ¼" (3 to 6 mm) by 8" (20.5 cm) to outline the stairs. Trim the strips to the length needed and fuse them in place. To finish off the stairs frame, fuse in place two vertical strips that extend from the top of the sand to the bottom of the house.

5 ways to make it your own

You can use the Beach House drawing to create your own sketch of a scene at your favorite beach. Make a rough sketch of the quilt you want to fuse in your sketchbook or on some scrap paper. Cut a piece of craft paper to the size you want your finished quilt to be, draw your quilt sketch out to scale with pencil, and then go over the lines with a permanent marker.

For your version of the Beach House Art Quilt, you could:

1 Remove one of the tree images and replace it with a sun in an upper corner of the quilt.

2 Add a surfboard leaning against one of the palm trees.

3 Make three smaller beach houses instead of one large one.

4 Use printed fabrics instead of solids, which will give the quilt a completely different look.

5 Piece together strips of different shades of blue fabric for the background.

Create Outlines

23 Cut three more ⅛" to ¼" (3 to 6 mm) outline strips along the width of the black fabric. Trim the strips to the lengths you need and fuse them to all of the elements of the quilt that don't already have outlines: the roof, the sides and bottom of the beach house, the trees, the sand, and the door.

24 Trim two black strips to the lengths needed for the house stilts and fuse them in place. I used ¼" (6 mm) wide strips.

25 Using straight stitches and black thread, sew through the centerline of each black outline strip and the windowpane strips. This secures the strips to the quilt.

Add Embellishments

26 Give your beach house a doorknob with a French knot.

Finish the Quilt

27 Finish the quilt by trimming it to 12" × 12" (30.5 × 30.5 cm). Add a false backing and binding. I bound my quilt using my four-strip binding technique (page 52), but you can bind it using any of the methods described in Chapter 6. Use the same backing fabric to sew a hanging sleeve. Add a label on the back of your quilt.

Layering a Fabric Collage

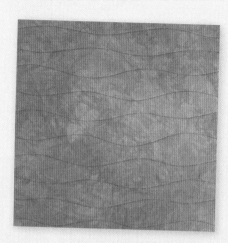

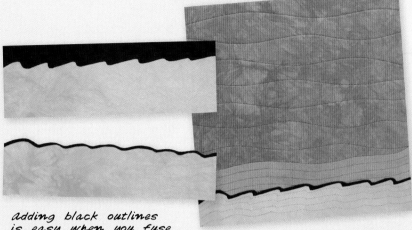

Quilt the base of your art quilt first, adding an all-over design to the sky-blue background.

Adding black outlines is easy when you fuse the primary fabric to the outline fabric, then trim the black back.

Fuse the foreground layers. If you're making a beach image, add first the sand, then the outlined water.

Use the cookie-cutter technique to making radiating outlines, such as palm treetops.

Fuse the middle ground layers. In a beach scene, start with the tree trunks, then add the outlined treetops.

Finally, add the focal point of the art quilt. For the Beach House, fuse the house, roof, window, and steps and stilts in place. Add the final outline pieces last.

Fuse your art quilt one piece at a time, adding new details with each layer. Quilt each element as you go, using the shapes of each piece as guides for your stitching.

laundry day
ART QUILT

This easy-to-make clothesline wall hanging is a great beginner project for exploring art quilting. It's also a terrific way to use small scraps of pre-fused fabrics that you have left over from previous quilt projects. The design is relatively simple, giving you an opportunity to experiment with both free-motion and straight-stitch quilting. You can easily size it up or down to accommodate your wall space.

supplies

Laundry Day drawing enlarged 434 percent

27" × 33" (68.5 × 84 cm) piece of blue fabric for the background

1 fat quarter of brown fabric for the tree trunks and laundry basket

½ yd (45.5 cm) of green fabric for the treetops and grass

11 different fabric scraps, each about 6" × 8" (15 × 20.5 cm), for the clothing

27" × 33" (68.5 × 84 cm) piece of muslin for the base

27" × 33" (68.5 × 84 cm) piece of wool felt for the batting

1 yard (91.5 cm) of coordinating fabric for the backing and hanging sleeve

2 packages of Mistyfuse fusible web

25" (63.5 cm) piece of string or yarn

9 small buttons or beads to embellish the clothing

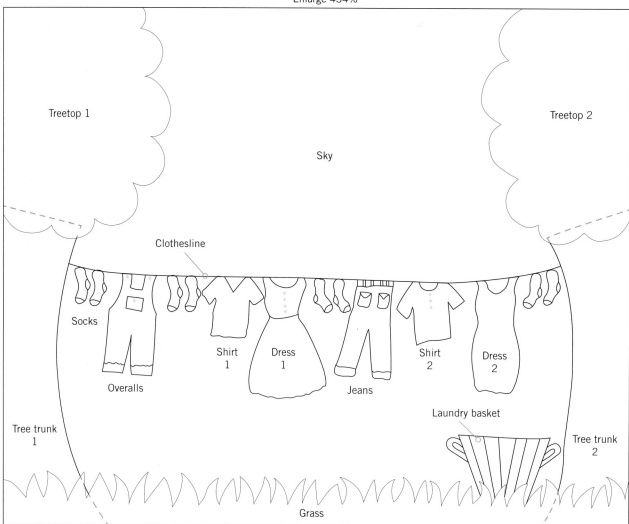

Prepare Pattern Pieces and Fabrics

1   Enlarge the drawing of the Laundry Day Art Quilt 434 percent so that it measures 24" × 30" (61 × 76 cm). You can use this design as a pattern and make this quilt exactly as shown, or you can sketch your own design elements on the enlarged drawing. You might want to add a sun, clouds, shrubs instead of grass, or different types of clothing hanging from the clothesline.

2   Trace the drawing using tracing paper and a black marker. Cut the tracing apart on the marked lines to create your pattern pieces.

Before adding the clothing on my pattern drawing, I did some rough sketches on scrap paper. This saved me from having to erase details on my drawing. If you want to add new items of clothing, draw those pieces on scrap paper, cut them out, and tape them to your drawing. This is a great way to work out the number and sizes of the pieces of clothing before committing them to your pattern drawing.

3   Apply fusible web to the wrong side of all of your fabrics, including the muslin.

Quilt the Background

4   Fuse the 27" × 33" (68.5 × 84 cm) piece of muslin to one side of the 27" × 33" (68.5 × 84 cm) piece of wool felt. Fuse the 27" × 33" (68.5 × 84 cm) piece of blue background fabric to the other side of the wool felt batting.

5 Quilt the background, then trim the quilt sandwich to 24" × 30" (61 × 76 cm). I free-motion quilted a random meandering pattern (page 38).

I like to quilt my background at this point before adding any additional imagery. It's easier to free-motion quilt when you don't have to sew around any of the collage design elements. Quilting the background before any imagery is fused on top also means that quilting lines will be unbroken, reducing the number of times you have to stop and start lines of quilting. There will be fewer thread tails to pull to the back when you're done.

In this quilt, much of the background will show. Consider your quilting design carefully. I like to keep my quilting simple, and I always use a thread color that closely matches the color of the background fabric. I want the quilting to blend into the background, not become a focal point.

Fuse the Trees

6 Using your pattern pieces, place the treetop and trunk shapes on the green and brown fabrics right side up. Cut the pieces out. Fuse the trees in place on the background, referring to the master drawing for placement **(figure 1, page 74)**.

7 Quilt the trunks and treetops, using their shapes to guide your stitching lines.

I used a series of straight stitches to quilt the trunks, spacing the lines of stitches about ½" (1.3 cm) apart. I quilted the treetops by following their shapes. After quilting the images, I outlined each one using a small zigzag stitch. This adds a bit of texture and visual interest.

> **QUILTING TIP** *It is easier to zigzag stitch on a curved shape if you set a fairly narrow stitch width. Stitch very slowly.*

Add the Laundry Basket and the Grass

8   With the pattern pieces right side up, cut out the grass from the green fabric and place it on the background, but do not fuse it in place yet. Cut out the laundry basket from the brown fabric and place it on the background behind the grass. Remove the grass and set it aside. Fuse the basket in place.

9   Quilt the laundry basket, and then zigzag stitch around the outer edges. I quilted a pattern that echoed the shape of the basket.

10   Replace the grass piece and fuse it in place **(figure 2)**.

11   Quilt the grass either with straight stitches or free-motion stitching. I echo quilted it by following the shapes of the blades of grass.

Add the Clothesline and Clothes

12   To create the clothesline, use a chalk marker to draw a line from one tree to the other. Couch (page 44) the piece of string or yarn on top of the chalk line.

Alternatively, you could fuse a thin strip of fabric or a ribbon between the trees.

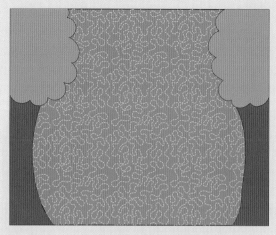

figure 1 - Fuse the trees to the background.

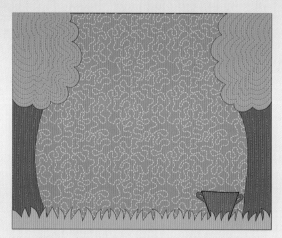

figure 2 - Fuse the grass and basket over the trees.

figure 3 - Add the clothesline and clothing last.

13 Use the pattern pieces to cut out and create the clothing to hang on the laundry line **(figure 3)**.

Although I drew socks on the original sketch, I left them off the quilt. When I cut them out of fabric, I didn't like the way they looked. I also originally had two different styles of dresses. The simpler straight dress didn't have the right look when I cut it out of fabric, so I just used one dress style. Don't ever feel that your original sketch must be followed exactly—sometimes, what looks good on paper doesn't translate well in fabric.

14 Play with the placement of the dresses, shirts, pants, and other items of clothing hanging on the clothesline. Fuse them in place, then embellish them with details. I fused contrasting fabric pockets and cuffs on the pants and overalls.

Rather than quilting the clothes, zigzag stitch around the outside edges of each item.

Add Embellishments

15 Sew on additional details to the clothing, such as buttons, beads, or tiny bows, or embroider some details with contrasting embroidery floss. I added three small buttons each to the three dresses. Mine were ¼" (6 mm) in diameter, but use whatever you have on hand.

Finish the Quilt

16 Square up the edges of your quilt to measure 30" × 24" (76 × 61 cm). Add a false backing and binding. I bound my quilt using my four-strip binding technique (page 52), but you can bind it using one of the methods described in Chapter 6. Use the same backing fabric to sew a hanging sleeve. Finally, add a label to the back of your quilt.

5 ways
to make it your own

The Laundry Day drawing is just the start of a design that depicts a scene of a breezy, relaxing day. If you want to add your own details, start by drawing a rough sketch in your sketchbook.

Experiment with different elements in your sketch, such as:

1 Create a version in pastel-colored fabrics with baby clothing on the line. It will make a wonderful addition to a nursery.

2 Hang miniature quilts from the clothesline instead. This version would be a fun wall hanging in your studio.

3 Add a sun to shine down on your laundry line.

4 Change the treetop shapes to resemble the trees in your backyard. Keep the shapes simple so that you can easily quilt the trees.

5 Draw alternative items of clothing, such as t-shirts and tank tops, shorts and pants, skirts, boxer shorts, or towels and sheets.

supplies

The City Skyline drawing enlarged 714 percent

½ yd (45.5 cm) of blue fabric for the background

1 fat quarter of white fabric for the clouds

½ yd (45.5 cm) total of six different fabrics for the skyscrapers

1 yd (91.5 cm) of black fabric for the outlines and binding

Assorted fabric scraps for the windows and doors

1½ yd (1.3 m) of muslin for the base

33" × 43" (84×109 cm) piece of wool felt for the batting

1 yard (91.5 cm) piece of fabric for the backing and hanging sleeve

2 packages of Mistyfuse fusible web

6 small buttons for the doorknobs

the
city
skyline
ART QUILT

FINISHED SIZE *30" × 40" (76 × 101.5 cm)*

Don't limit yourself to using just solid, bright fabrics for your version of this quilt. Consider using a combination of bright prints with solids or make a gray-scale version using black, white, and gray tones. The billboard is a good opportunity for a sly joke or a bit of hometown charm.

The City Skyline Drawing
Enlarge 714%

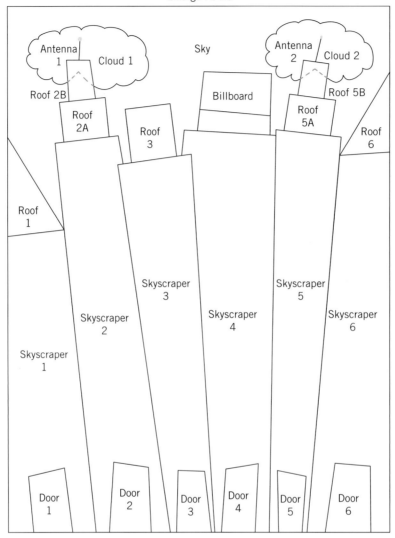

Prepare Pattern Pieces and Fabrics

1 Enlarge the drawing of the City Skyline Art Quilt 714 percent so that it measures 30" × 40" (76 × 101.5 cm). You can use this design as a pattern and make it as shown, or you can modify it by sketching buildings of your own design.

2 Trace the drawing using tracing paper and a black marker. You may find it helpful to use a long straight edge or ruler to trace your buildings. To make it easier to remember which roof goes with which building, number each set so you'll know

which piece goes where, as I did on the master drawing. If your tracing paper isn't large enough to make a single tracing, just trace your pattern pieces in sections. Cut the tracing apart on the marked lines to create your pattern pieces.

3 Cut a piece of black fabric 10" (25.5 cm) long and as wide as the fabric. Reserve it for the binding.

Apply fusible web to the wrong side of all of your fabrics, including the muslin and the remaining black fabric, which you'll use to outline the design elements.

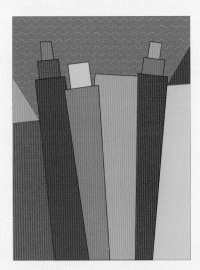

figure 1 - Fuse the buildings to the quilted background and muslin.

figure 2 - Add the doors to the quilted buildings.

figure 3 - Experiment with the placement of the windows.

Quilt the Background

4 Fuse the 33" × 43" (84 × 109 cm) piece of wool felt to the wrong side of the 33" × 43" (84 × 109 cm) piece of muslin.

5 Because very little of the sky in this quilt is going to show, use your pattern to cut the sky piece out of blue fabric, rather than using a piece of blue to cover the entire quilt top.

Use the top edges of the building to determine the shape of the sky piece, but add an extra ¼" (6 mm) to the bottom edge. This will make it easier to place the building pieces when you get to that step.

6 Quilt the sky area. For my quilt, I straight stitched horizontal, wavy lines across the sky. The lines were randomly spaced between ¾" and 1¼" (2 to 3.2 cm) apart.

Cut and Fuse the Buildings

7 Use your pattern pieces to cut out the buildings from your pre-fused fabrics. Fuse them in place on the quilt top **(figure 1)**.

8 Quilt the buildings using straight stitches, following the shape of each building.

I stitched vertical lines extending from the top of the buildings to the bottom, spacing them about ¼" to ½" (6 mm to 1.3 cm) apart. Alternatively, you can follow the outside edges of each building to repeat the shape inside the buildings to create a maze pattern.

9 Use your pattern pieces to cut out the doors from your fabric scraps. Fuse them in place **(figure 2)**.

10 Quilt the doors with lines of straight stitches in a pattern similar to that used for the buildings.

Create the Windows

11 Working on one skyscraper at a time, cut several wonky rectangles for the windows. The number of windows might be different for each building. Experiment with the placement of the rectangles on each building to make sure you have enough to fill the space. Do not fuse them in place **(figure 3)**.

Move the rectangles to an ironing surface, placing them right side up on top of a nonstick press sheet.

12 Cut several ⅛" to ¼" (3 mm to 6 mm) wide strips of black fabric along the width of the fabric. Use them to create the panes on the windows, referring to "Creating Four-Step Windows" on page 66.

13 Fuse the windows to the quilt top and then add the window outlines **(figure 4)**.

I like to extend my outline strips beyond the edges of the windows, but you could trim them flush if you prefer. Save any leftover black strips to outline the doors and buildings.

> **FABRIC COLLAGE TIP** *Instead of framing your windows with black strips, try using a different color. Or experiment using strips cut from a printed multicolored fabric or a black and white print.*

Make the Billboard

14 Using the pattern piece, cut out the square for the billboard. Fuse it in place on the quilt. Fuse ¼" (6 mm) wide black strips around the billboard, extending the right and left side strips down to the top of the building to attach the billboard to the roof.

> **DESIGN TIP** *The billboard installed on top of the skyscrapers is the perfect space for personalizing your quilt. For my version, I printed a digital sketch onto cotton inkjet printer fabric. Alternatively, you could scan one of your sketches into your computer and then print it out onto fabric, draw or paint directly onto a piece of fabric cut to the size of the billboard, or create a small fused collage the size of the billboard.*

Fuse the Clouds

15 Fuse the fat quarter of white fabric to a piece of muslin, then apply fusible web to the muslin. This prevents the blue sky fabric from tinting the clouds once they're fused to the quilt top.

16 To outline your clouds in black, place your cloud pattern pieces on the right side of your pre-fused black fabric. Trace two clouds with a chalk marker.

Refer to "Making Cookie Cutter Outlines" on page 64 as well as to **figure 5**. Beginning in the center of one of the traced black pieces, cut a small slit

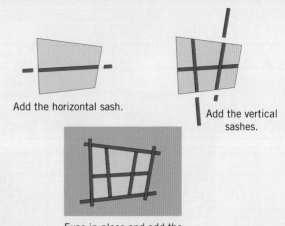

Add the horizontal sash.　　Add the vertical sashes.

Fuse in place and add the outer window trim.

figure 4 - Make enough windows to fill the buildings.

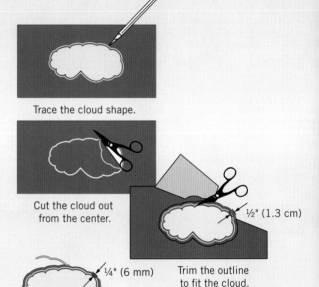

Trace the cloud shape.

Cut the cloud out from the center.

½" (1.3 cm)

Trim the outline to fit the cloud.

¼" (6 mm)

Fuse the outline to the cloud and trim to ¼".

figure 5 - Make black cookie-cutter outlines for the clouds.

figure 6 - Fuse the clouds behind the rooftops.

to insert your scissors. Cut just to the traced line, and then cut all around the shape on the traced line. Next, cut the outside edge of the black cloud shape ½" (1.3 cm) away from the traced line, following the shape of the traced line.

Repeat for the second cloud outline.

17 Fuse the black cloud outline shapes to the white fabric with muslin. Trim the outer edges of the black fabric to ¼" (6 mm) on each cloud.

Fuse the clouds in place on the quilt top **(figure 6)**.

18 Use free-motion meandering stitches to quilt the clouds, or use the outline of the clouds to quilt a pattern that echoes the shape of the clouds.

Add the Antennas

19 Add a radio antenna to each of the tops of two buildings. Fuse two ⅛" × 1¾" (3 × 4.5 cm) strips of black fabric in place, referring to the pattern drawing for placement.

Outline the Skyscrapers

20 Cut twenty strips of pre-fused black fabric ⅛" to ¼" (3 to 6 mm) wide along the width of the fabric. Fuse the strips to the outside edges of all of the skyscrapers, windows, and doors to create outlines (except where the binding will overlap).

21 Stitch a single line down the center of each black strip, including the cloud outlines and the radio antennas, to secure the outlines to your quilt top.

Add Embellishments

22 Add doorknob details to the doors. I used ¼" (6 mm) buttons, but you could use beads or embroider French knots with contrasting embroidery floss.

Finish the Quilt

23 Square up the edges of your quilt if necessary to measure 30" × 40" (76 × 101.5 cm). Add a false backing and binding. I bound my quilt using my four-strip binding technique (page 52), but you could use any of the methods described in Chapter 6. Use the same backing fabric to sew a hanging sleeve. Finally, add a label to the back of your quilt.

5 ways
to make it your own

The City Skyline Art Quilt can be made to resemble the skyscrapers in your town— or any of the world's big cities with an easily recognizable skyline, such as San Francisco, New York, London, or Paris. Or build a dream city from scratch.

Sketch your favorite skyscrapers and:

1 Consider using a combination of bright prints and solid fabrics.

2 Try making a gray-scale version using only black, white, and gray tones.

3 Instead of using rectangles for the windows, experiment with circles, squares, or even retro half-moon windows.

4 Use a dark navy blue and create a night sky. Replace the clouds with small glass seed beads to look like twinkling stars.

5 Add a blimp or a skywriting airplane above the skyscrapers.

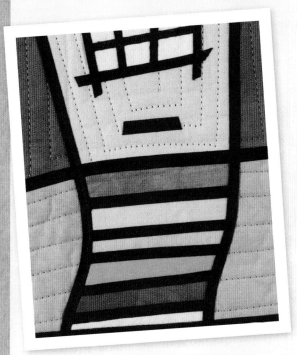

my house
ART QUILT

This charming art quilt makes a wonderful housewarming or wedding gift. The simple shapes make it easy to size up or down to fit into your friends' decor. You can customize it further by adding their address on the mailbox or match the color of the fabric house to their house.

supplies

My House drawing enlarged 390 percent

22"×22" (56×56 cm) piece of blue fabric for the background

1 fat quarter of brown fabric for the tree trunk

1 fat quarter of green fabric for the treetops and grass

1 fat quarter of yellow fabric for the sun

¾ yd (68.5 cm) of black fabric for the outlines and binding

½ yd (45.5 cm) total of fabric scraps for the house, garage, walkway, driveway, and mailbox

22"×22" (56×56 cm) piece of muslin for the base

22"×22" (56×56 cm) piece of wool felt for the batting

1 yard (91.5 cm) of coordinating fabric for the backing and hanging sleeve

2 packages of Mistyfuse fusible web

1 small button for the doorknob

My House Drawing
Enlarge 390%

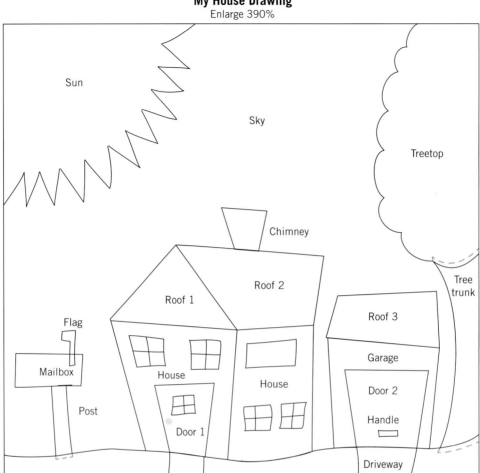

Prepare Pattern Pieces and Fabrics

1   Enlarge the drawing of the My House Art Quilt 390 percent so that it measures 20" × 20" (51 × 51 cm). You can use this design as a pattern and make the quilt as shown, or you can sketch some customized drawings over the design.

2   Trace the drawing using tracing paper and a black marker. Cut the tracing apart on the marked lines to create your pattern pieces.

3   Cut an 8" (20.5 cm) wide piece of black fabric along the width of the fabric and reserve it for the binding.

Apply fusible web to the wrong side of each of your fabrics, including the muslin, and the remaining black fabric, which will be used to outline the design elements.

Quilt the Background

4   Fuse the 22" × 22" (56 × 56 cm) piece of wool felt to the wrong side of the 22" × 22" (56 × 56 cm) piece of muslin. Fuse the 22" × 22" (56 × 56 cm) piece of blue background fabric to the other side of the wool felt.

5   Quilt the entire background. I free-motion quilted a simple meandering quilting pattern (page 38).

6   Trim the quilt sandwich to 20" × 20" (51 × 51 cm).

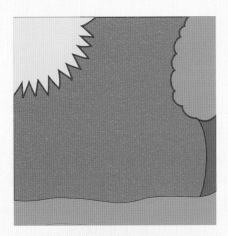

figure 1 - Fuse the foreground pieces to the background.

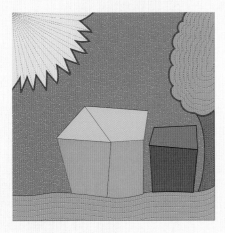

figure 2 - Fuse the middle ground images to the background.

figure 3 - Layer the doors on the quilted buildings.

Add the Grass, Sun, and Tree

7 Use your pattern pieces to cut out the grass and the tree trunk. Fuse them in place.

8 To add a black outline around the treetop, trace the treetop pattern on the right side of the black fabric with a chalk marker.

Refer to "Making Cooking Cutter Outlines" on page 64. Beginning in the center of the traced shape, cut just to the traced line. Cut all around the shape on the traced line. Cut the outside edge of the black treetop shape ½" (1.3 cm) away from the traced line, repeating the shape of the traced line.

9 Place the black treetop outline on top of your green fabric and fuse it in place. Cut out the treetop from the green fabric by trimming the outer edge of the black outline to ¼" (6 mm).

Fuse the treetop onto the top of the tree trunk.

10 Use your pattern pieces to cut out the sun. Outline it with black fabric using the same cookie-cutter technique that you used to outline the treetop. Fuse the sun in place **(figure 1)**.

11 Quilt the grass, the tree, and the sun.

I used a free-motion meandering stitch on the grass. For the treetop, I free-motion stitched lines that echoed the scalloped edge, then I quilted the tree trunk with a series of vertical straight stitches spaced about ¼" (6 mm) apart. To quilt the sun, I sewed straight lines radiating from the outer edge of the quilt toward the outside edge of the sun.

Fuse the House and Garage

12 Use your pattern pieces to cut out the house, garage, and the two roofs from your fabric scraps. Fuse them in place **(figure 2)**, referring to the master drawing for placement.

13 Quilt the house, garage, and roofs with straight stitches. Follow the shapes of the elements, spacing your stitched lines about ½" (1.3 cm) apart. I stitched mine in a maze pattern that mimics the shapes.

14 Use your pattern pieces to cut out the doors and chimney. Fuse them in place **(figure 3)**.

15 Quilt the doors and the chimney with straight stitches, following their shapes as you stitch. Keep your stitched lines ½" (1.3 cm) apart.

16 Use your pattern pieces to cut out the mailbox, flag, and post. Fuse them in place.

17 Quilt the mailbox and post with simple straight stitches.

Build the Windows

18 To create the five windows for the house and its front door and for the garage door, cut out five different wonky rectangular shapes. Note that the window above the house's door is a slightly wider rectangle.

> **FABRIC COLLAGE TIP** *Making all of the windows a different color is a great way to bring in some additional colors. Cut each window separately by hand into a slightly different shape to add to the wonky charm of the house.*

19 Cut ten ⅛" × 6" (3 mm × 15 cm) strips from the black fabric. Place them horizontally and vertically over the windows to create the panes. Trim the strips to match the width and length of the windows and fuse them in place. Refer to "Creating Four-Step Windows" on page 66.

20 Create one window with curtains. Cut three pieces of pre-fused fabric, each with one gently-curved edge. Fuse a ⅛" (3 mm) wide black strip over the outside edges of these curtain pieces **(figure 4)**.

21 Fuse the windows in place on the house, its door, and the garage door. Fuse ⅛" (3 mm) wide black strips around the outside edges of the windows to frame them. To achieve the same look as the sample quilt, extend the outline strips beyond the outside edge of the windows.

Create the Pathways

22 To make the walkway and driveway, cut fourteen strips in random colors and widths ranging from ¾" to 1½" (2 to 3.8 cm) from your pre-fused fabric scraps. Lay them on top of a piece of parchment paper, overlapping each strip about a ¼" (6 mm). Press with a hot iron to fuse them into one piece of striped fabric **(figure 5)**.

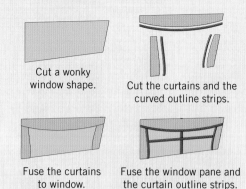

Cut a wonky window shape.

Cut the curtains and the curved outline strips.

Fuse the curtains to window.

Fuse the window pane and the curtain outline strips.

figure 4 - Hang a curtain in the window of the house.

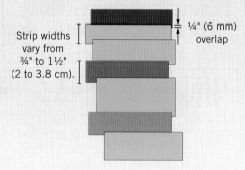

Strip widths vary from ¾" to 1½" (2 to 3.8 cm).

¼" (6 mm) overlap

figure 5 - Overlap strip edges and fuse in place.

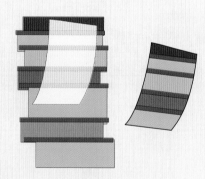

figure 6 - Cut walkway and driveway from the fused pieces.

figure 7 - Fuse the striped pathways to the quilt.

23 Cut several more strips of ¼" (6 mm) wide black fabric and trim them to fit the length of your colored strips. Fuse them over the edges where the strips overlap.

24 Using the tracing paper patterns, cut both of the pathways out from the striped pieces **(figure 6)**. Fuse them in place on the quilt **(figure 7)**.

Outline the Elements

25 Cutting across the width of the pre-fused black fabric, cut four ⅛" to ¼" (3 to 6 mm) wide strips. Use them to outline the house, garage, roofs, pathways, mailbox, post, grass, chimney, and just the left-hand side of the tree trunk. Fuse the strips in place.

26 Using straight stitches, sew through the centerline of each black strip to secure the outlines.

Add Embellishments

27 This art quilt needs very little embellishment. Simply sew a small button on the door for a doorknob. I used a ¼" (6 mm) button, but you can use whatever you have in your stash.

28 Fuse a small scrap from one of your outline strips to the garage door to make a door handle.

Finish the Quilt

29 Add a false backing, then trim the quilt to 20" × 20" (51 × 51 cm). Add the binding. I bound my quilt using my four-strip binding technique (page 52), but you could use any of the methods that are described in Chapter 6. Use the same backing fabric to sew a hanging sleeve. Finally, add a label to the back of your quilt.

5 ways to make it your own

The My House Art Quilt should look like your house, not my house! You can easily personalize it in a variety of ways to reflect where you live—or where your friends live, if you're making this as a gift.

In addition to choosing real-life house colors and adding your address, you can also:

1 Make it a winter scene. Use white for snow in place of the green grass and replace the window on the front door with a festive wreath.

2 Take out the mailbox and add a white picket fence to the background.

3 Shrink down the garage into a dog-house and make a small sign with your dog's name on it.

4 Leave out the garage and the walkway. String a clothesline from the corner of the house to the tree or fill in the space with a wonky car and a driveway.

5 Make the house a two-story home with dormer windows.

wonky
house
lane
TABLE RUNNER

supplies

Wonky House Lane drawing
enlarged 690 percent

½ yd (45.5 cm) of blue fabric for the
background

¼ yd (23 cm) of green fabric for the
grass

1¼ yd (114.5 cm) of black fabric for
the outlines and binding

8 fat quarters for the houses,
windows, chimneys, and doors

21" x 45" (53.5 x 114.5 cm) piece of
muslin for the base

21" × 45" (53.5 × 114.5 cm) piece of
wool felt for the batting

21" × 45" (53.5 × 114.5 cm) piece of
fabric for the backing

2 packages of Mistyfuse fusible web

7 small buttons for the doorknobs

FINISHED SIZE *42" × 18" (106.5 × 45.5 cm)*

A table runner can be displayed on a
tabletop or, with a sleeve on the back,
can work equally well hanging on a wall.
Customize the size of this runner to fit your
table—or a specific section of wall—or make
a series of placemat-sized mini quilts for a
complete table setting.

Wonky House Lane Drawing
Enlarge 690%

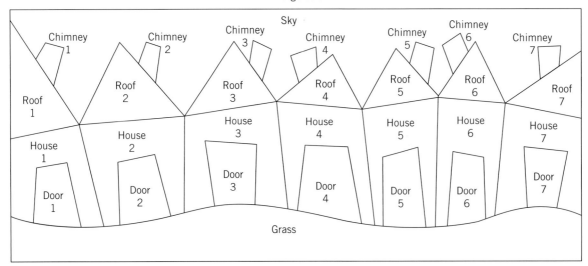

FABRIC TIP *If you prefer, use fabric scraps to create the windows, doors, and chimneys. After you have traced the drawing and cut out the pattern pieces, you can raid your scrap basket.*

Prepare Pattern Pieces and Fabrics

1 Enlarge the drawing of the Wonky House Lane Table Runner 690 percent so that it measures 18" × 42" (45.5 × 106.5 cm). You can use this as a pattern to make the quilt as shown, or you can sketch new elements to make the lane resemble your street.

2 Trace the drawing on tracing paper with a black marker. Label all of the traced elements so you'll know which pieces will make up each house after you cut apart the tracing. Cut the tracing on the marked lines to create your pattern pieces.

3 Cut an 8" (20.5 cm) wide piece from the length of the black fabric. Reserve it for the binding.

Apply fusible web to the wrong sides of all of your fabrics, including the muslin and the remaining black fabric.

Quilt the Background

4 Fuse the 21" × 45" (53.5 × 114.5 cm) piece of muslin to the 21" × 45" (53.5 × 114.5 cm) piece of wool felt.

5 Place your pattern pieces for the sky and the grass right side up on the blue and green fabrics. Cut the pieces out and then fuse the sky and grass in place on the quilt top.

6 Quilt the sky and grass.

I free-motion quilted a meandering pattern (page 38) for the sky. For the grass, I used straight stitches and followed the top edge of the grass shape, randomly spacing my lines of stitches about ½" (1.3 mm) apart.

Fuse the Houses

7 With right sides facing up, use your pattern pieces to cut out the houses and roofs. Fuse them in place on the quilt top, matching the numbers on the roof pattern pieces with the numbers on the house pattern pieces (**figure 1**).

FABRIC COLLAGE TIP *You may find it easier to cut and fuse all of the house bottoms in place first and then add the roofs.*

8 Quilt the houses and roofs with straight stitches, following their square and triangular shapes to guide your lines of stitches. Space your quilting lines about ½" (1.3 cm) apart. There's no need to worry about being exact because randomness will add to the wonky charm of the finished work.

Add the Doors and Chimneys

9 With right sides facing up, use the pattern pieces to cut out the doors and chimneys from your fabric scraps. Fuse them in place on the houses. You could change the chimney shapes to resemble stovepipe chimneys on some of the houses (**figure 2**).

5 ways
to make it your own

The Wonky House Lane Table Runner is a cheerful street with one- and two-story houses. Depending on the fabrics you choose and the features you give your houses, you could make it look very different.

To personalize this table runner, you could:

1 Omit the grass at the bottom of the quilt and extend your houses all the way to the bottom edge.

2 Add a tree to each side of the row of houses or insert a tree between each house.

3 Leave some space between each house and add some shrubs, fire hydrants, or street lamps. Instead of using green for grass, use gray for a road.

4 Use ric rac or a small-scale black-and-white polka dot print for the outline strips.

5 Change the chimney shapes to stovepipe chimneys.

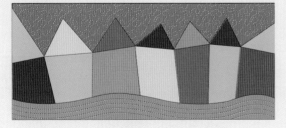

figure 1 - Make sure the correct roof pieces are fused to the houses.

figure 2 - Stovepipe chimneys are a whimsical alternative for the roofs.

10 Use straight stitches to quilt the doors and chimneys, following their shapes as you stitch. Space the stitched lines about ½" (1.3 cm), allowing them to go a little wonky.

Create the Windows

11 Cut 21 small wonky squares and rectangles from your pre-fused fat quarters or fabric scraps to make your windows. Try them out on the houses before you add the windowpanes. Place them on your ironing surface right side up.

12 Cut twelve ⅛" to ¼" (3 to 6 mm) wide strips from the length of the black fabric. Refer to "Creating Four-Step Windows" on page 66, and fuse strips horizontally and vertically onto the window shapes to create windowpanes. Trim the strips so that they don't extend beyond the outside edges of the windows.

13 Fuse the windows in place on the houses and then fuse additional black strips around the outside edges of the window to frame them. I like to extend my outline strips beyond the edges of the windows, but you could trim them flush if you prefer.

Outline the Houses

14 Cut 12 more ⅛" to ¼" (3 to 6 mm) wide strips of black fabric. Fuse them in place to outline the houses, doors, windows, and chimneys, trimming the strips to fit each element.

15 Using straight stitches, sew through the centerline of all of the black strips to secure the outlines.

Add Embellishments

16 Add a doorknob detail to each of the doors. On my table runner, I used ¼" (6 mm) buttons, but you could use beads or embroider French knots with contrasting embroidery floss instead.

Finish the Table Runner

17 Add a false backing to the table runner, then trim it to 18" × 42" (45.5 × 106.5 cm). Use the reserved black fabric to bind the edges with my four-step binding technique (page 52) and add a label to the back. If you want to use your table runner as a wall hanging, add a hanging sleeve with fabric from your stash.

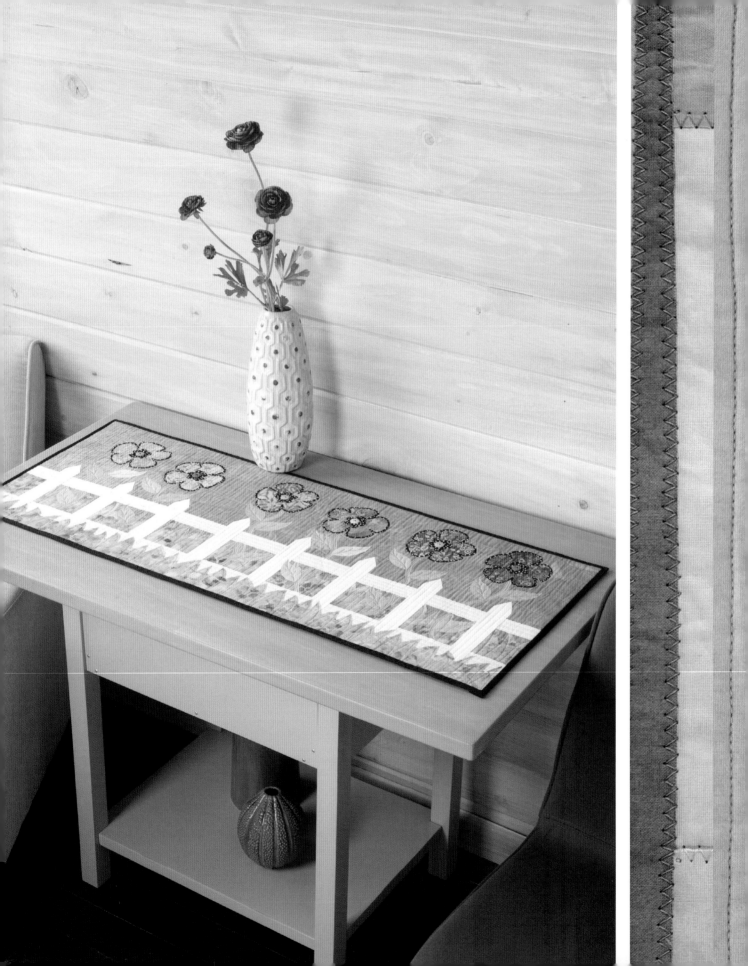

the
flower
garden
TABLE RUNNER

Add a bouquet of whimsy to your table with this cheerful table runner inspired by a bright sunny day. Or use it as a bureau topper to bring a bright spot of quilted color to your guest room.

supplies

The Flower Garden drawing enlarged 690 percent

⅝ yd (57 cm) of blue fabric for the background

1 fat quarter of white fabric for the fencing

½ yd (45.5 cm) of green batik fabric for the grass

6 fat quarters of various batik fabrics for the flowers

1 fat quarter of polka dot fabric for the flower centers and outlines

1 fat quarter of green fabric for the stems and leaves

20" x 44" (51 × 112 cm) piece of wool felt for the batting

1½ yd (1.3 m) of muslin for the base

1¼ yd (91.5 cm) black fabric for the binding

20" × 44" (51 × 112 cm) piece of coordinating fabric for the backing

2 packages of Mistyfuse fusible web

6 medium buttons for the flower centers

The Flower Garden Drawing
Enlarge 690%

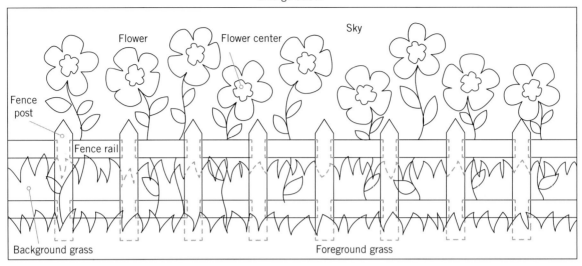

Prepare Pattern Pieces and Fabrics

1 Enlarge the drawing of the Flower Garden Table Runner 690 percent so that it measures 18" × 42" (45.5 × 106.5 cm). You can use this drawing as a pattern to make this quilt exactly as shown or sketch your own designs on top to reflect your own garden.

> **DESIGN TIP** *The pattern drawing has nine flowers, but I ended up using only six flowers on my table runner. I used the drawing as a guide for the scale and general placement of the elements. When it came time to fuse the flowers and leaves in place, I didn't worry about where I had drawn them in and placed them wherever I wanted to on the actual quilt. You can have as many (or as few) flowers as you wish.*

I used the Accuquilt GO! Funky Flowers die to create my flower shapes for this runner, but you could replace them with your own drawings of your favorite flowers.

2 Trace the drawing on tracing paper with a black marker. Cut the tracing apart on the traced lines, including separating the fence posts and rails. Use the pieces as patterns to cut your fabric pieces.

3 Apply fusible web to the wrong sides of your fabrics for the background, flowers, leaves, fence posts and rails, and grass, as well as the muslin.

Quilt the Background

4 Fuse the 20" × 44" (51 × 112 cm) piece of muslin to one side of the wool felt. From the blue fabric, cut a 20" × 44" (51 × 112 cm) piece. Fuse it to the other side of the wool felt batting.

5 Quilt the entire background. I straight stitched horizontal, wavy stitches for the sky. The lines are randomly spaced between ¾" to 1¼" (2 to 3.2 cm) apart.

Add the Background Grass

6 Use the pattern piece to cut out the tall background grass from the green batik fabric. Fuse it in place **(figure 1)**, referring to the master drawing for placement.

7 Quilt only the background grass using straight stitches. Start from the bottom edge and weave up to the top edge of the grass. Pivot at the top points of the grass, then stitch back to the bottom edge. This echoes the shapes of the grass blades.

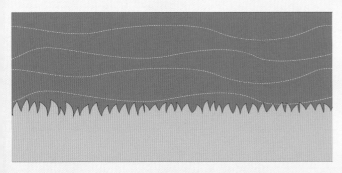

figure 1 - Fuse the background grass to the quilted sky.

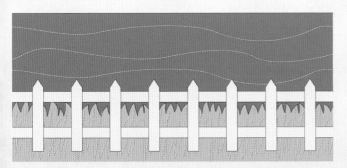

figure 2 - Fuse the picket fence pieces to the quilted background grass.

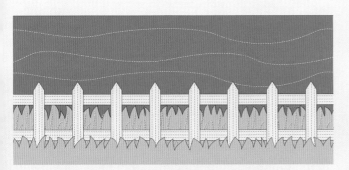

figure 3 - Fuse the foreground grass over the quilted fence.

Create the White Picket Fence

8   Using the pattern pieces, cut out the fence post and rail pieces from white fabric. Note that the posts and rails need to be cut slightly longer than what will actually be visible. Fuse them in place over the background grass **(figure 2)**, referring to the master drawing for placement.

9   Quilt the fence posts using vertical columns and the rails using horizontal rows of straight stitches, about ¼" to ⅜" (6 mm to 1 cm) apart.

Add the Foreground Grass

10 Use the pattern piece to cut out the shorter piece of foreground grass from the same green batik fabric. Align the bottom straight edge of the grass with the bottom straight edge of the background. Fuse it in place over the bottom edge of the fence **(figure 3)**.

11 Quilt the foreground grass in the same way you quilted the background grass, following the curved lines of the grass.

Add the Stems, Flowers, and Leaves

12 To give the flowers a contrasting outline, trace the flower pattern pieces on the right side of the pre-fused polka dot fabric with a chalk marker. Leave at least 1" (2.5 cm) between tracings.

Refer to "Making Cookie Cutter Outlines" on page 64. Cut out the center of one of the traced shapes, snipping just to the traced line. Cut out the shape on the chalk line. Cut around the outside of the flower shape, creating a ½" (1.3 cm) wide outline for the flower.

Repeat the process to cut out the outlines for your remaining flowers.

13 Use the pattern pieces to cut out the flowers from batik fabric. If you want to use the same flower shape for each flower, cut several flowers out at once.

14 Place the polka dot flower outlines on top of the batik flower fabric and fuse them in place. Leave at least ½" (1.3 cm) between the outlines for trimming. Trim the outer edges of the outlines to ¼" (6 mm).

15 Fuse the flowers to the background, floating them above the picket fence. Space them a little unevenly across the width of the background and at slightly different heights.

16 Using the pattern pieces, cut out smaller flower shapes from the polka dot fabric. Fuse one to the center of each flower.

17 Use straight stitches to sew through the center-lines of the flower outlines to secure them to the background.

18 Add stems to the flowers by cutting wavy strips of solid green fabric ¼" (6 mm) wide. Make sure they're long enough to extend from the bottom of your flowers to the bottom of the quilt. Place them on the quilt and then cut off and discard the pieces that extend in front of the fence.

Check that the sections of each stem look as though they line up behind the fence. Fuse the stems in place.

figure 4 – Fuse all of the flower pieces in place, placing them in a naturally uneven way across the fence.

19 Cut the leaves from the same green fabric and fuse them in place to complete the flowers. You may want a few of the leaves to overlap the fence posts and rails **(figure 4)**.

20 Stitch along the centerlines of the stems to secure them in place with matching green or a variegated thread. Add vein details to the leaves by free-motion stitching, straight stitching, or hand stitching in a darker green color.

Add Embellishments

21 Add one button to the center of each flower. I used 1" (1.3 cm) buttons. Alternatively, fill the center with French knots tied with a contrasting color of embroidery floss or embellish your flowers with beads.

Finish the Table Runner

22 Add a false backing, then trim the edges of your table runner to measure 18" × 42" (45.5 × 106.5 cm). Add the binding. I used my four-strip binding technique (page 52), but you can bind your table running using any one of the methods described in Chapter 6. Add a label to the back. If you'd rather use the table runner as a wall hanging, use fabric from your stash to make a hanging sleeve.

5 ways
to make it your own

This is a straightforward design, but one you can easily personalize with small touches that make big changes in the final table runner. Show your love for your garden by using fabrics and images that are just your own.

Alter this table runner in simple ways:

1 Change the shape of the flower. Tulips or daisies are easy to draw, or you could sketch one from your imagination.

2 Remove the picket fence and plant your flowers in different-colored flowerpots.

3 Add some butterflies, ladybugs, or birds to the garden.

4 Instead of a fence, create a trellis with grape vines.

5 Create a winter garden scene using white fabric for snow and fill the garden with holly branches, winterberry, or heather.

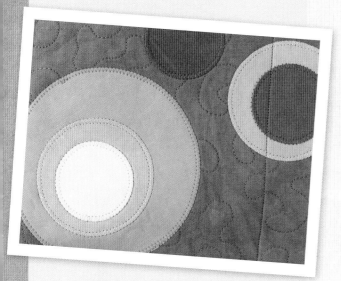

supplies

1 yd (91.5 cm) of dark gray fabric for the shell

1 yd (91.5 cm) of light gray fabric for the lining

½ yd (45.5 cm) of black fabric for the binding

1¼ yd (114.5 cm) total fabric scraps in a variety of colors for the appliqué circles

1 yd (91.5 cm) of wool felt for the batting

2 packages of Mistyfuse fusible web

14" (35.5 cm) leather handbag handles with pre-punched holes

Waxed twine, upholstery thread, or tapestry thread

Tapestry needle

2", 3", and 5" (5 cm, 7.5 cm, and 12.5 cm) circle templates

Point turner

full circle
TOTE BAG

FINISHED SIZE *12.5" × 12.5" × 4.5" (31.5 × 31.5 × 11.5 cm)*

This stylish tote bag goes together very quickly and has a nice roomy interior. There's plenty of space to carry all of your things, whether it's to the office, out for a day of shopping, or off to a meeting at your quilting guild.

Quilt the Exterior Fabric

1   Cut a piece of dark gray fabric and a piece of wool felt that each measures 36" × 28" (91.5 × 71 cm). Apply fusible web to the wrong side of the dark gray piece and fuse it to the wool felt batting.

2   Quilt the entire piece. I free-motion quilted a random meandering pattern (page 38).

> **QUILTING TIP** *Quilt the bag shell with a free-motion pattern. This is a great opportunity to practice free-motion quilting and to concentrate on keeping your stitch length consistent and uniform.*

Cut the Exterior Pieces

3   From the quilted exterior fabric, cut out seven panel pieces for the outside of the tote bag. Label the back of each piece as you cut them:

Piece 1: Front panel, 13" × 13" (33 × 33 cm)

Piece 2: Back panel, 13" × 13" (33 × 33 cm)

Piece 3: Right side panel, 13" × 5" (33 × 12.5 cm)

Piece 4: Left side panel, 13" × 5" (33 × 12.5 cm)

Piece 5: Bottom panel, 13" × 5" (33 × 12.5 cm)

Piece 6: Front pocket panel, 13" × 7" (33 × 18 cm)

Piece 7: Back pocket panel, 13" × 7" (33 × 18 cm)

Appliqué the Shell Pieces

4   Apply fusible web to the wrong side of each of the fabric scraps for the circles.

5   Trace circles of three sizes ranging from 2" to 5" (5 to 12.5 cm) onto the pre-fused fabric scraps. I made thirty-five 2" (5 cm) diameter circles, eighteen 3" (7.5 cm) diameter circles, and three 5" (12.5 cm) diameter circles.

> **DESIGN TIP** *I cut the circles for my tote bag with a die cutter, but you can trace circular shapes that you find around your home, such as glassware, small bowls, mugs, and soda cans, onto your fabrics.*

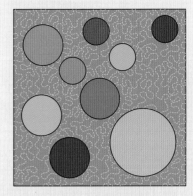

Piece 1: Front panel

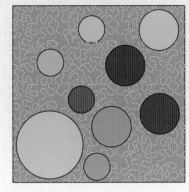

Piece 2: Back panel

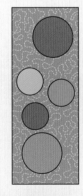 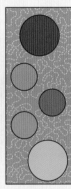 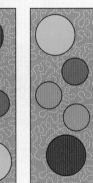

Piece 3:   Piece 4:   Piece 5:
Right side panel   Left side panel   Bottom panel

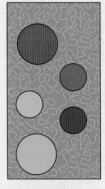 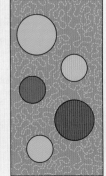

Piece 6:   Piece 7:
Front pocket panel   Back pocket panel

figure 1 - Fuse the circles to the quilted exterior pieces.

6 Cut out the traced circles and experiment with their placement on each of the seven exterior panels (**figure 1**). Try layering a few of the larger circles with some smaller circles in contrasting colors.

7 When you're happy with their placement on each of the panels, fuse the circles in place.

Using zigzag stitches and matching thread, sew around the outside edge of each circle.

Line and Bind the Pocket Panels

Note: All seam allowances are ¼" (6 mm) unless otherwise noted.

8 Place the appliquéd front pocket panel (piece 6) and back pocket panel (piece 7) on your work surface, right side down. Cut two pieces of light gray fabric each measuring 13" × 7" (33 × 18 cm). Apply fusible web to the wrong side of each piece, and then fuse one to the wrong side of each of the pocket panels. This will create a nice finish for the insides of the pockets.

9 Cut two strips of black fabric, each 2" × 13" (5 × 33 cm), to use as binding for the top edges of the two pocket panels.

10 Pin one strip, right sides together, to the top edge of one of the pocket panels and sew them together. Press the strip, turn the pocket panel over, and fold the binding strip in half along the long edge. Press with an iron to set the crease.

Fold the binding strip over the top edge of the pocket toward the back, pin, and hand sew the binding with slip stitches (page 53) to the back of the pocket.

Repeat with the second binding strip and pocket panel.

5 ways to make it your own

Circles aren't the only way to embellish this tote bag! Think of the gray shell of the bag as a blank canvas, which you can customize in a million different ways. Stitch up a bag for each of your favorite hobbies or experiment with a variety of new colorways.

Using stencils, cutting dies, or your own sketches, you could:

1 Instead of circles on your tote bag, use the no-reverse appliqué method on page 25 to create letters and cover the bag with your initials.

2 Customize your bag with other easy-to-cut geometric shapes, such as squares or triangles.

3 Using the flower shape from the Flower Garden Table Runner (page 92), cover the tote bag with flowers, swap in a vinyl handle, and use it as a garden tool tote.

4 For a beach tote, apply the Beach House Art Quilt (page 60) design elements to add a row of beach houses to the outside pockets.

5 Instead of using fused circles, embellish the panels of the tote with colorful buttons. Be sure to use a sturdy thread or floss and keep the buttons at least 1" (2.5 cm) away from the edges so they don't get caught in any seam allowances.

Sew the Pocket Panels

11 Mark a line down the center of the front pocket panel with a chalk marker. Place it on the front panel (piece 1), aligning the raw edges along the bottom and the sides **(figure 2)**. Sew along the marked line to secure the front pocket to the front panel. Back stitch at the top edge of the pocket to secure it.

Repeat with the back pocket panel and back panel (piece 2).

Assemble the Tote Bag

12 Pin the right side panel (piece 3) and the left side panel (piece 4) to the bag front, right sides together, aligning the 13" (33 cm) edges. Sew the side panels to the bag front, stopping ¼" (6 mm) from the bottom edges of the panels **(figure 3)**.

13 With the wrong side of the bottom panel (piece 5) facing up, draw parallel lines ¼" (6 mm) away from each of the 5" (12.5 cm) long sides. With right sides together, pin the bottom panel to the front panel, aligning the long edges.

The bottom panel will extend beyond the left and right edges by ¼" (6 mm). Match your drawn lines with the seams that join the side panels to the front panel. Pin and sew the bottom panel in place, beginning and ending at the drawn lines. **(figure 4)**.

14 With right sides together, pin the side panels to the back panel.

It's easier to do this if you pin and sew one seam at a time, rather than pinning all of the edges and then sewing. Start by placing the front panel on your work surface right side up with the side panels opened out. Align the back panel with one of the side panels along the 13" (33 cm) edge, right sides together. Pin and sew them together **(figure 5)**.

Repeat with the second side panel.

15 At this point, the bottom panel is attached to only the front of the bag **(figure 6)**. With right sides together, pin the remaining long edge of the bottom panel to the back panel. Align the bottom panel so that the drawn lines match the seams that join the side panels to the back panel. Sew the bottom panel to the back panel, similar to Step 13 **(figure 7)**.

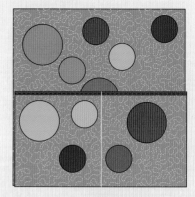

figure 2 - Sew the pocket panels to the front and back panels.

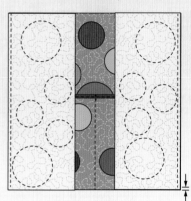

figure 3 - Attach the side panels to the front panel.

¼" (6 mm)

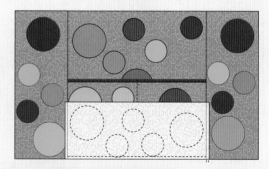

figure 4 - Make sure the bottom panel overlaps the side panels ¼" (6 mm) on each side.

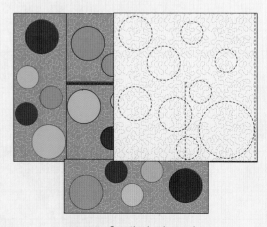

figure 5 - Sew the back panel on one side seam at a time.

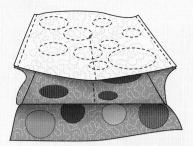

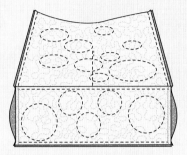

figure 6 - Sew the bottom panel to the front panel.

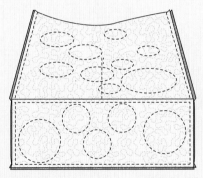

figure 7 - Sew the bottom panel to the back panel.

figure 8 - Finish attaching the bottom of the bag by sewing the side seams.

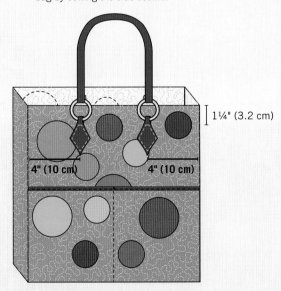

figure 9 - Stitch the bag handles centered on the front of the bag.

16 With right sides together, pin and sew the side panels to the bottom panel, beginning and ending at the seams that you stitched previously **(figure 8)**.

17 Clip the bottom corners to remove some of the bulk. Turn the shell right side out and gently push out the corners with the point turner.

Attach the Handles

18 Sew the handles onto the front and back panels of the bag, centering them side to side and at least 1¼" (3.2 cm) from the top edge. This leaves enough room to sew the lining and binding to the top edge in a later step. Mine are spaced about 4" (10 cm) from each side panel seam **(figure 9)**.

I used 14" (35.5 cm) leather handles that have tabs with pre-punched sewing holes. If your handles don't have the holes already punched, then use an awl to punch the sewing holes. Use a sturdy thread such as waxed linen, tapestry thread, or upholstery thread to sew the handles to the bag.

Cut Out the Lining

19 Cut seven lining pieces from the light gray lining fabric. Label the back of each piece as you cut them:

Piece 1: Front lining panel, 13" × 13" (33 × 33 cm)

Piece 2: Back lining panel, 13" × 13" (33 × 33 cm)

Piece 3: Right side lining panel, 13" × 5" (33 × 12.5 cm)

Piece 4: Left side lining panel, 13" × 5" (33 × 12.5 cm)

Piece 5: Bottom lining panel, 13" × 5" (33 × 12.5 cm)

Piece 6: Front pocket lining panel, 13" × 13" (33 × 33 cm)

Piece 7: Back pocket lining panel, 13" × 13" (33 × 33 cm)

Sew the Lining

20 Fold the front pocket lining panel (piece 6) in half and press with a hot iron to set a crease. Use a chalk marker to draw a line down the center from the creased fold to the bottom raw edge.

Place the front lining panel (piece 1) on your work surface, right side up. Place the front pocket lining panel on top of the front lining panel, aligning the raw edges along the bottom and the sides. Sew along the marked line to secure the pocket to the front lining panel **(figure 10)**. Back stitch at the top edge of the pocket to secure it.

Repeat to sew the back pocket lining panel (piece 7) to the back lining panel (piece 2).

21 Pin, then sew the side lining panels to the front lining panel, right sides together, as you did for the bag shell in Step 12.

22 Following Step 13, pin and sew the bottom and front lining panels together.

23 With right sides together, pin, then sew the back lining panel to the side lining panels.

24 With right sides together, pin the remaining long edge of the bottom lining panel to the back lining panel, as you did in Step 15. Sew the panels together, beginning and ending at the drawn lines.

25 Finally, with right sides together, pin and sew the side lining panels to the bottom lining panel, beginning and ending at the seams that you stitched previously. Clip the bottom corners to remove some of the bulk and gently push out the corners with the point turner.

Assemble the Tote Bag

26 With wrong sides together, slip the lining into the bag **(figure 11)**. Align the side seams of the lining with the side seams of the exterior of the bag. Sew both pieces together along the top edge.

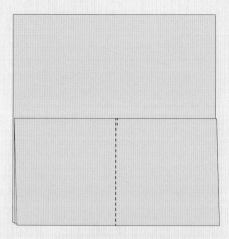

figure 10 - Sew the front pocket lining panel to the front lining panel.

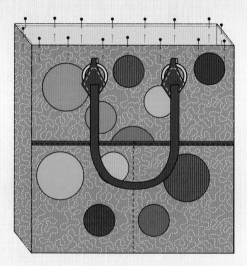

figure 11 - Insert the lining into the bag, wrong sides together.

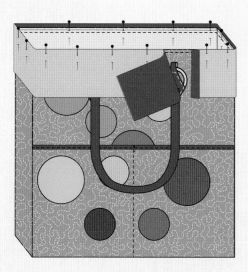

figure 12 - Pin the binding fabric to the top edge, right sides together.

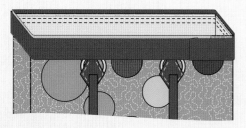

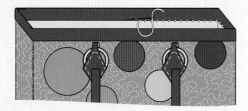

figure 13 - Fold the binding, then secure it inside the bag with slip stitches.

Bind the Top Edge

27 Cut a piece of black fabric 3" × 36½" (7.5 × 92.5 cm). With the wrong side facing up, fold one short end of the strip over ½" (1.3 cm) and press to set a crease.

28 Beginning in the center of the right side panel, with right sides together, align the edges and pin the folded short end of the binding to the top edge of the bag. Sew the binding strip to the top edge of the bag using a ½" (1.3 cm) seam allowance **(figure 12)**.

When you get to the point where you started sewing, trim the excess binding to allow for a 1" (2.5 cm) overlap and tuck the end underneath the folded end of the binding. Continue sewing about 1" (2.5 cm) beyond your starting point. Make sure that as you stitch over your beginning stitches the stitches overlap.

29 Fold the binding in half along the top edge and press it with a hot iron to set the crease. Then fold the binding to the inside of the bag. Pin and hand sew the binding with slip stitches **(figure 13)**.

stay chic

QUILTED BACKPACK

supplies

1 yd (91.5 cm) of tan faux suede fabric for the bottom panel, flap, and straps

3 fat quarters of turquoise and brown solids and batiks for the front and back panels

1 yd (91.5 cm) of tan fabric for the lining

¼ yd (23 cm) of turquoise batik for the front flap binding

1 yd (91.5 cm) of wool felt for the batting

1 package Mistyfuse fusible web

1" (2.5 cm) swivel snap clip and D-ring

1 medium-size decorative button

Fourteen ¼" (6 mm) grommets and installation tool

1 yd (91.5 cm) of brown leather cord

1 barrel-shaped cord lock

Binder clips

Point turner

FINISHED SIZE *16" × 14" (40.5 × 35.5 cm)*

At first glance, this quilted backpack may look like a difficult project, but it's deceptively easy to make. The striped body of the bag is created quickly with fused strips, so there are no tedious seams to sew and press open. Just take it one step at a time, and before you know it, you'll have a new backpack to carry your quilt supplies in.

Create the Striped Panels

1 The main body of the bag is made up of two striped panels—one for the front, the other for the back. Each measures 17" × 11" (43 × 28 cm).

To create the striped panels, first cut two pieces of wool felt measuring 18" × 12" (45.5 × 30.5 cm). (The extra is to allow for shrinkage when quilting.)

2 Apply fusible web to the wrong sides of the three fat quarters.

From one fat quarter, cut and reserve a 12" × 12" (30.5 × 30.5cm) piece that will be used to line the front flap.

Cut the remaining fat quarters into 28 strips, each measuring 1½" × 12" (3.8 × 30.5 cm).

3 Alternating the solids and the batik fabrics, arrange fourteen strips on top of each of the two pieces of batting, overlapping each strip by ¼" (6 mm), to create the stripes **(figure 1)**. Fuse the strips in place.

4 Zigzag stitch along each overlapping edge, as I did, or quilt the two striped panels in an allover pattern.

Trim each panel to 17" × 11" (43 × 28 cm), then set them aside while you create the bottom panels.

Create the Contrasting Panels

5 Cut a piece of tan faux suede fabric and a piece of wool felt, each 8" × 36" (20.5 × 91.5 cm). Clip them together with binder clips.

6 Quilt the bottom piece. I used straight stitches and quilted a grid pattern on the diagonal.

7 Cut the quilted panel into two pieces, each measuring 7" × 17" (18 × 43 cm).

> **FABRIC TIP** When working with faux suede, always use a piece of muslin or cotton as a press cloth. Do not touch the iron directly to its surface or you will flatten the pile. If faux suede is unavailable, swap in a different faux leather, denim, or linen. Almost any fabric can be used in this project because it's stabilized with the wool felt batting. Also, you can use polyester or cotton webbing instead of making straps.

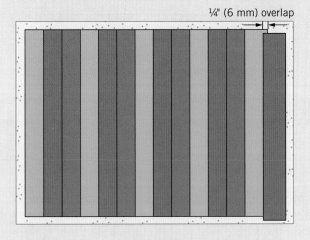

¼" (6 mm) overlap

figure 1 - Fuse the strips to make the striped panels.

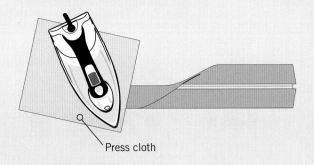

Press cloth

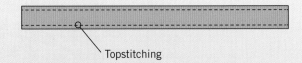

Topstitching

figure 2 - Make the straps by folding, pressing, and topstitching the faux suede strips.

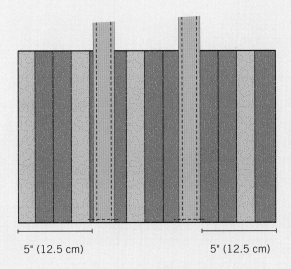

5" (12.5 cm)   5" (12.5 cm)

figure 3 - Center and stitch down
the shoulder straps.

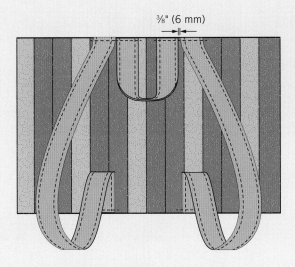

⅜" (6 mm)

figure 4 - Stitch the carry handle
between the shoulder straps.

Sew the Straps

Note: *All seam allowances are ½" (1.3 cm) unless
otherwise noted.*

8 Sew 5 separate 1½" (3.8 cm) wide straps. If you
want your backpack to have longer (or shorter)
shoulder straps, just increase (or decrease) the
length of these straps accordingly.

Cut out from the remaining faux suede:

Piece 1: Right shoulder strap, 5½" × 26" (14 × 66 cm)

Piece 2: Left shoulder strap, 5½" × 26" (14 × 66 cm)

Piece 3: Carry handle, 5½" × 14" (14 × 35.5 cm)

Piece 4: Flap swivel snap clip strap, 4" × 6"
(10 × 15 cm)

Piece 5: Bottom D-ring strap, 4" × 6" (10 × 15 cm)

9 Fold each faux suede strip in half lengthwise and
press the fold in the center, making sure you use
a press cloth to protect the fabric. Fold each long
edge to the center pressed line. Fold the strips in
half again lengthwise to enclose the raw edges .
Use binder clips to hold the folded strap in place.
Topstitch along the long edges of each strap using
a ¼" (6 mm) seam allowance **(figure 2)**.

Assemble the Shell

10 Place one of the striped panels on your work
surface right side up—this will be the back of
the shell.

Aligning the raw edges, pin the short ends of the
two shoulder straps to the 17" (43 cm) long bottom
edge of the striped panel, 5" (12.5 cm) from each
side. Sew the bottom edge of the straps in place
using a ¼" (6 mm) seam allowance **(figure 3)**.

11 Align the raw edges of the opposite ends of the
shoulder straps with the top edge of the panel, 5"
(12.5 com) from each side. Sew using a ¼" (6 mm)
seam allowance.

12 Pin the carry handle strap to the top edge of the
panel in the space between the shoulder straps.
I placed each end of my carry handle strap ⅜"
(1 cm) away from the edge of the shoulder straps.
Sew using a ¼" (6 mm) seam allowance **(figure 4)**.

13 Place the other striped panel on your work surface, right side up—this will be the front of the shell.

Measure and mark the center of the bottom edge. Slip the D-ring onto the bottom D-ring strap. Fold the strap in half so that the short raw edges are aligned, and then pin the strap to the center of the bottom edge of the front panel, aligning the raw edges. Sew using a ¼" (6 mm) seam allowance **(figure 5)**.

14 Place the striped back panel on your work surface right side up. Pin one of the quilted faux suede bottom panels to the bottom edge of the striped back panel, aligning the long raw edges. Pin and sew together.

Repeat with the striped front panel and second quilted faux suede bottom panel.

15 With right sides together and aligning the raw edges all around, pin the front and back panels together. Sew the two side seams, and then sew the bottom seam.

16 To box the bottom edge of the backpack, open the seam allowances at one corner and fold so that the side seams are aligned with the bottom seam. Pin them together. With chalk, mark a line perpendicular to the seam 2" (5 cm) from the point. Stitch on the marked line and trim off the corner **(figure 6)**.

Repeat with the second bottom corner.

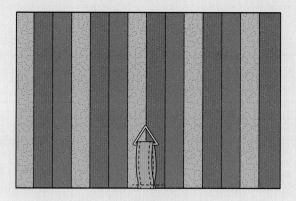

figure 5 - Center and stitch down the bottom D-ring strap.

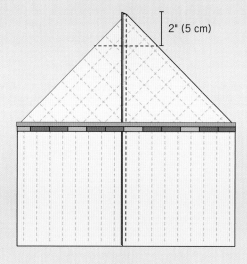

2" (5 cm)

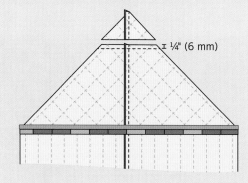

¼" (6 mm)

figure 6 - Box both bottom corners of the backpack shell.

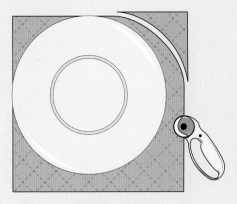

figure 7 - Use a salad plate to trace the curved edge on the front flap.

figure 8 - Sew the binding to the front flap.

Create the Front Flap

17 Cut a piece of wool felt and a piece of faux suede 12" × 12" (30.5 × 30.5 cm). Clip or pin the faux suede to the wool felt and quilt. I used straight stitches and quilted a grid on the diagonal.

18 Fuse the 12" × 12" (30.5 × 30.5 cm) piece of fabric to the other side of the wool felt, and then trim it to measure 11" × 11" (28 × 28 cm).

19 Round two corners of one side of the square. Place a salad plate on the flap and trace the curved edge. Trim the corners off by carefully cutting on your traced line **(figure 7)**.

20 From your front flap binding fabric, cut a strip 2" × 30" (5 × 76 cm).

21 With the right sides together (the faux suede side is the right side of the flap) and the raw edges aligned, clip or pin the binding strip to the flap. Start at one corner and then pin it around the curved edge to the opposite corner **(figure 8)**. Sew the binding in place using a ¼" (6 mm) seam allowance.

22 Fold the binding in half along the top edge and press it with a hot iron to set the crease. Fold the binding to the inside of the flap and hand sew it in place with slip stitches (page 53).

Attach the Flap

23 With right sides together, pin the front flap to the back panel of the shell, aligning the raw edges and centering the flap between the left- and right-hand side seams. Sew the flap to the shell using a ¼" (6 mm) seam allowance.

24 Slip the swivel snap clip onto the flap swivel snap clip strap and fold the strap in half so that the short raw edges are aligned.

With the lining side of the flap facing up, center the strap on the curved edge. The raw edges of the strap should be placed 2" (5 cm) below the outside bound curved edge of the flap. The folded end of the strap should extend about 1" (2.5 cm) beyond the outside curved edge **(figure 9)**.

Sew the strap in place. Sew the decorative button to the front side of the flap to hide the stitching on the lining side made from attaching the swivel snap clip strap.

25 Turn the shell right side out.

Sew the Lining

26 Cut two 18" × 18" (45.5 × 45.5 cm) pieces from the light gray lining fabric. Pin the pieces right sides together, aligning the raw edges. Sew along three sides, leaving a 4" (10 cm) opening for turning **(figure 10)**.

27 Box the bottom edge of the bag lining as in Step 16. Use the point turner to gently push out and shape the corners.

Complete the Backpack

28 Make sure the backpack shell is right side out and the lining is wrong side out. With right sides together, slip the shell into the lining **(figure 11)**. Align the side seams of the shell and lining and the raw edges at the top, then pin.

29 Carefully turn the backpack right side out through the opening in the lining. Sew the opening closed with slip stitches.

Press the lining and the shell, using a press cloth to protect the faux suede.

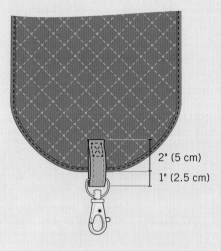

2" (5 cm)
1" (2.5 cm)

figure 9 - Center and attach the swivel snap clip strap.

4" (10 cm)

figure 10 - Leave an opening in the lining to turn the backpack right side out.

figure 11 - Insert the backpack shell into the lining, then pin.

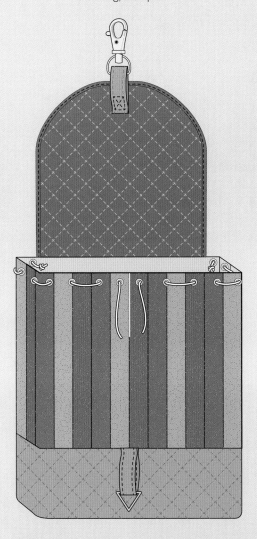

figure 11 - Thread the drawstring through the grommets, leaving the tails in the front.

Install the Drawstring

30 Evenly mark fourteen spots around the top edge of the backpack, spacing them 1¼" to 1½" (3.2 cm to 3.8 cm) apart and ¾" (2 cm) from the top. Marks should be 1" (2.5 cm) away from the side seams and equidistant from the centerline of the front panel.

Following the manufacturer's instructions, install one grommet at each marked spot. Alternatively, sew buttonholes at the marked spots.

31 Cut the leather cording in half and make a large knot on one end of each piece. Beginning at the grommet near one side seam and with the knot on the inside of the backpack, thread one length through seven of the grommets, ending at the front of the bag **(figure 12)**.

Repeat with the second length of cording on the other side of the bag. Slip the two unknotted ends of the cording through the cord lock. Tie the two cords together with a knot, leaving 1½" (3.8 cm) long tails.

tri-fold
E-FOLIO

This e-reader cover is fast and easy to make, and it provides stylish protection for your device. It's designed to fit a Kindle, but you can size it up or down to fit whatever e-reader you want to use it for, including an iPad or other tablet computer. This cover uses a variety of fabrics, so it's a great way to use some of your favorite quilting scraps.

supplies

½ yd (45.5 cm) of light gray fabric for the exterior

½ yd (45.5 cm) of dark gray fabric for the lining and outlines

6 to 8 fabric scraps for the stripes, each measuring at least 4" × 10" (10 × 25.5 cm)

14" × 8½" (35.5 × 21.5 cm) piece of stiff interfacing, such as Timtex, Peltex 70, or Stiffy, for the base

14" × 8½" (35.5 × 21.5 cm) piece of wool felt for the batting

1 package of Mistyfuse fusible web

14" (35.5 cm) piece of round elastic cord

Awl

Make the Base of the Cover

1 Fuse the 14" × 8½" (35.3 × 21.5 cm) piece of stiff interfacing to one side of the 14" × 8½" (35.5 × 21.5 cm) piece of wool felt.

Cut a 14" × 8½" (35.3 × 21.5 cm) piece from the light gray fabric. Fuse it to the other side of the wool felt. This is the right side of the e-reader cover.

2 Apply fusible web to the wrong side of your dark gray fabric as well as to the fabric scraps that you'll use to make the stripes.

> **SIZING TIP** *These instructions will accommodate a 5" × 7½" (12.5 × 19 cm) Kindle.*
>
> *To make a cover for a different device, adjust the measurements accordingly. For a sleeve for an iPad that measures 7½" × 9½" (19 × 24 cm), you need to start with a piece of stiff interfacing that is 10½" × 19" (26.5 × 48.5 cm). That equals 1" (2.5 cm) longer than the height of the device and twice its width plus 4" (10 cm) to account for the pocket on the inside of the cover.*

Add Embellishments

3 Cut six to eight wonky strips from your fabric scraps. Cut the strips at least 1" to 2" wide and 9" long (2.5 to 5 cm wide and 23 cm long), leaving some wider at one end than the other.

4 Fuse the strips to the light gray fabric with the stripes running from top to bottom. Allow some of the gray fabric to show through between your stripes **(figure 1)**.

5 Quilt the stripes and the light gray sections. I used straight stitches and threads that matched each stripe, repeating the angled lines of the stripes.

Add the Outlines

6 The number of stripes you added to the light gray fabric will determine the number of dark gray outline strips you need. Cut enough ¼" × 9¼" (6 mm × 23 cm) strips to add outlines to each edge of your stripes.

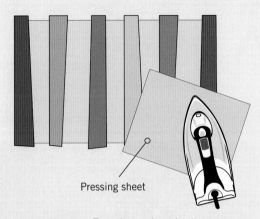

Pressing sheet

figure 1 - Fuse the wonky strips to the base fabric.

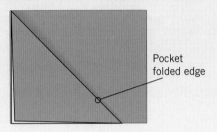

Pocket folded edge

figure 2 - Align the pocket panel with the folded edge in the center.

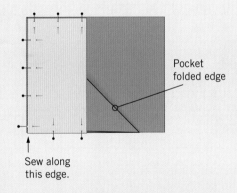

Pocket folded edge

Sew along this edge.

figure 3 - Sandwich the pocket panel between the inside panels.

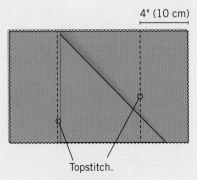

4" (10 cm)

Topstitch.

figure 4 - Add topstitching to create fold lines on each side.

7 Fuse the outline strips in place and trim. Using a matching thread, straight stitch down the centerlines of each outline strip to secure them.

Create the Lining

8 The lining of the cover includes a pocket to hold an e-reader. To make the lining, cut three rectangles of dark gray fabric:

Piece 1: Inside right panel, 10" × 8½" (26.5 × 21.5 cm)

Piece 2: Inside left panel, 4¼" × 8½" (11.5 × 21.5 cm)

Piece 3: Pocket panel, 8½" × 8½" (21.5 × 21.5 cm)

9 Fold the pocket panel (piece 3) in half diagonally and press.

10 Place the inside right panel (piece 1) on your work surface right side up. Place the folded pocket panel (piece 3) on top, aligning the raw edges along the left and bottom edges of the inside right panel **(figure 2)**. Pin in place.

11 With right sides together, pin the inside left panel (piece 2) on top of the pocket panel, aligning the left raw edges and the top and bottom edges **(figure 3)**.

12 Sew the three pieces together along the 8½" (21.5 cm) edges using a ¼" (6 mm) seam allowance. Press the seam allowance open.

13 Measure the inside lining to make sure that it is 14" (35.5 cm) wide. Trim any excess from the right side.

14 Fuse the lining to the wrong side of the striped front cover panel.

Topstitch the Cover

15 Set your sewing machine for a wide zigzag stitch or a satin stitch. I used dense zigzag stitches on my e-folio. Zigzag or satin stitch around all four edges of the sleeve to secure the lining to the cover as well as provide a neat finish.

FINISHING TIP *When finishing the edge of any project with a zigzag stitch, don't try to lay down too thick a stitch on the first pass. Set your stitch density a little looser than you think it should be and make several passes around the cover. You'll get better coverage and a more polished finish.*

16 With the lining side facing up (and the folded edge of the pocket at the top), topstitch over the seam that joins the pocket piece to the inside left side of the lining. Keep in mind that this stitching will show on the exterior of the cover, so choose a coordinating bobbin thread.

17 With the lining side facing up (and the folded edge of the pocket at the top), use a chalk marker to draw a line 4" (10 cm) from the right edge of the lining. Sew with a straight stitch over the marked line, using a bobbin thread that coordinates with the fabric on the exterior of the cover **(figure 4)**.

18 Fold the cover along both lines of stitching you just made and press.

Install the Elastic Closure

19 The 14" (35.5 cm) long elastic cord will help keep your e-reader cover closed and your device secure. You may have to adjust this length depending on how thick your finished cover is. It's better to work with a piece that is too long because you can adjust it once you have installed it.

20 Place the cover on your work surface, lining side up with the folded edge of the pocket at the top. Use a sharp awl to poke two holes just to the left of the topstitching that runs between the edge of the pocket and the left side of the lining. Center these holes between the top and bottom edges of the cover about ⅛" to ¼" (3 to 6 mm) apart.

21 From the outside of the cover, thread one end of the elastic cord through each hole. Knot each end of the elastic cord on the inside and then pull the elastic cord to the outside.

flower power
FABRIC JOURNAL

There's something special about writing or sketching in a book that you've made yourself. Fill this small journal with your ideas, sketches, and drawings for new art quilts. When the pages are filled up, you can easily take the signatures out and sew in fresh new ones.

supplies

The Flower Power Fabric Journal appliqué drawing enlarged 135 percent

1 fat quarter of turquoise fabric for the exterior

½ yd (45.5 cm) of purple fabric for the lining

7" × 7" (18 × 18 cm) scrap of pink fabric for the flower

7" × 8" (18 × 20.5 cm) scrap of green fabric for the stems and leaves

9" × 14" (23 × 35.5 cm) piece of stiff interfacing, such as Timtex, Peltex 70, or Stiffy, for the base

9" × 14" (23 × 35.5 cm) piece of wool felt for the batting

1 package of Mistyfuse fusible web

1 small decorative button

45 pieces of 8½" × 11" (21.5 × 28 cm) paper

1 yd (91.5 cm) twine, embroidery floss, or perle cotton

15" (38 cm) length of round elastic cord

Tapestry needle

Flower Power Fabric Journal Appliqué Drawing
Enlarge 135%

Make the Cover

1 Fuse the 9" × 14" (23 × 35.5 cm) piece of stiff interfacing to the 9" × 14" (23 × 35.5 cm) piece of wool felt. Cut a 9" × 14" (23 × 35.5 cm) piece of the turquoise exterior fabric, and then fuse it to other side of the wool felt batting.

2 Quilt the background using a free-motion swirl pattern (page 38) or choose another organic quilting pattern.

3 Apply fusible web to the red and green fabric scraps that will become the flower, stem, and leaves on the front of your journal.

Add Embellishments

4 Enlarge the Flower Power Fabric Journal Appliqué drawing 135 percent, and cut out the pieces. To make the flower petals, use the pattern pieces or cut by hand six triangles from your pre-fused quilting scraps. Make them roughly

figure 1 - Arrange the flower petals, stem, and leaves on the cover.

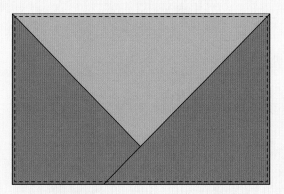

figure 2 - Fold two pieces of lining fabric into pocketsand stitch around the outside.

2" (5 cm) long and 1" (2.5 cm) wide at the top. Your triangles do not have to be all the same size—if you cut them randomly, the wonkiness of the cut will add to the charm of the journal cover.

Place the journal cover on your work surface, right side facing up with the 14" (35.5 cm) side laying horizontally. The right half of the shell is the front of the journal cover.

Experiment with the placement of the flower petals on the cover.

5 Using the pattern pieces, cut a ¼" (6 mm) wide curved stem and two leaves from the green fabric. Place them on the front cover, spanning the space between the petals and the bottom edge **(figure 1)**. When you're happy with the arrangement of the flower petals, stem, and leaves, fuse them in place.

6 With straight stitches, sew three lines along the stem and three lines on each flower petal, echoing the shapes of the outsides edges.

On each leaf, sew a line of stitches that extends from the bottom of the cover to the top and then sew a few veins. Sew the decorative button in the center of the flower. I used a 1" (2.5 cm) button, but choose a coordinating one from your stash.

Create the Lining and Pockets

7 Cut a piece of purple lining fabric 9" × 14" (23 × 35.5 cm). Fuse it to the inside of the journal cover.

8 Cut two more pieces from the purple lining fabric, each 9" × 9" (23 × 23 cm). Fold each one in half on the diagonal, wrong sides together, and press. These are the inside pockets of the journal.

9 Pin one pocket to each side of the lining, matching the side and bottom raw edges. The bottom edges of the pockets will overlap along the bottom center. Stitch all four of the outside edges **(figure 2)**.

Finish the Edges

10 Set your sewing machine for a wide zigzag stitch or a satin stitch. Zigzag around the edges of the sleeve to secure the lining to the cover of the journal. Make several passes around the outside of the journal to provide a nice, neat finish. I set my zigzag stitches so that they are about ¼" (6 mm) wide.

Add the Signatures

11 To add pages to the journal, fold each of the 45 pieces of paper in half. They should measure 5½" × 8½" (14 × 21.5 cm). Divide the pages evenly into three piles (or signatures) and then nest the folds together in each pile.

> **PAPER TIP** *You can use any paper you like for the inside of your journal. Plain white printer or copier paper works just fine if you're only planning on writing with pen or pencil. For working with watercolors, markers, paint, or any type of wet media, choose a heavier weight paper, such as watercolor or mixed media paper.*
>
> *You can use a single type of paper or a combination, but keep in mind that if you use a heavier type of paper, you may have room for fewer sheets.*

12 Make a hole-punching template for poking the holes in the pages. Fold an extra piece of paper in half and make four marks in the fold. Starting from the top, make a mark at 1", 2½", 6", and 7½" (2.5, 6.5, 15, and 19 cm). Label them 1 to 4 with 1 being at the top **(figure 3)**.

13 Place your hole-punching guide in one of the signatures and punch through the holes using a sharp awl **(figure 4)**.

Repeat with the other two signatures and then set them aside.

Punch Holes in the Shell

14 With the journal cover oriented so that the 14" (35.5 cm) side is placed horizontally on your work surface and the lining side is facing up, use a chalk marker to draw a line down the center from the top edge to the bottom edge. Mark another two lines ¼" (6 mm) away on either side of the center line.

15 Unfold the hole-punching guide and place it on the first marked line, aligning the fold with the marked center line and centering it between the top and bottom edges. Use a sharp awl to punch the four holes in the journal shell **(figure 5)**.

Repeat this on the other two marked lines.

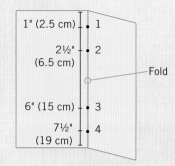

figure 3 - Make a template for punching the holes in the paper.

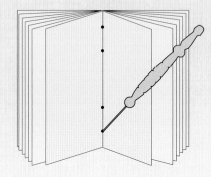

figure 4 - Use the template to punch holes in the paper, one signature at a time.

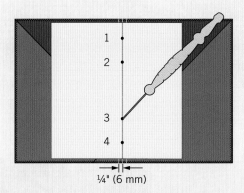

figure 5 - Use the same template to punch holes in the cover.

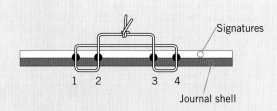

figure 6 - Stitch the signatures to the cover.

16 If you want your journal shell to have an elastic closure, punch two additional holes along the center line. Punch them ⅛" (3 mm) apart centered between the top and bottom edges.

Sew in the Signatures

17 Thread a tapestry needle with an 18" (45.5 cm) length of twine, embroidery floss, or perle cotton. Align one signature with the set of holes farthest from the left inside edge of the journal. Starting from the inside of the journal, insert the needle into hole 2 of the signature and then insert it in the corresponding hole 2 in the journal cover. Pull the needle and twine to the exterior of the journal shell, leaving a 6" (15 cm) tail on the inside.

18 Insert the needle in hole 1 of the exterior of the journal and bring the needle and twine back to the interior, through the corresponding hole 1 in the signature. Pull the twine so that it is taut with the exterior of the journal shell.

19 Insert the needle and twine in hole 4 in the signature and through the corresponding hole 4 in the journal shell. Pull the needle and twine to the exterior of the of the journal shell.

20 Finally, insert the needle in hole 3 in the exterior of the journal and bring the needle and twine back to the interior, through the corresponding hole 3 of the signature. Pull the twine so that it is taut with the exterior of the journal cover.

Tie the two tails together with a knot. Trim the tails to ½" to ¾" (1.3 to 2 cm) long **(figure 6)**.

21 Repeat this process to sew the additional two signatures into the remaining sets of holes in the cover. Note that when you are sewing in the signatures along the center line, you should ignore the two holes that you punched for the elastic closure.

Add an Elastic Closure

22 Working from the outside of the journal cover, thread one end of the elastic cord through one of the center holes and the other end of the elastic cord through the other center hole. Knot the ends on the inside of the journal shell and then pull the elastic loop on the outside around the journal to keep it closed.

5 ways to make it your own

A quilted journal is a blank canvas—inside and out. Its diminutive size makes it the perfect space to experiment with different types and styles of imagery and various embellishments with multimedia.

This geometric flower is just one way to embellish the journal. To make your journal more personal, you could:

1 Give the front cover some shimmer by adding foil embellishments to the flower petals or leaves.

2 Add some additional color and interest to the pages by fusing scraps of fabric directly to the paper. It's a great way to preserve the last, tiny scraps of your most cherished fabrics.

3 Mix into your signatures a few colored pages, old maps, vintage book pages, or even pages made from brown craft paper.

4 Fuse some stationery envelopes to a page or two to create little hidden pockets within the pages.

5 Add some beading to the spine of the journal by threading beads as you sew in the signatures. When the needle is on the outside of the journal, thread three or four beads before you pass the needle back through to the inside.

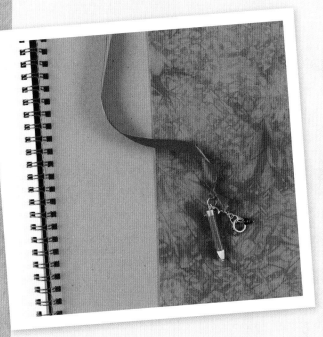

supplies

1 fat quarter of green fabric for the cover

2 fat quarters of purple fabric for the lining and pockets

6 to 8 different 8"×8" (20.5×20.5 cm) fabric scraps for the letters and stripes

19½"×12" (49.5×30.5 cm) piece of stiff interfacing, such as Timtex, Peltex 70, or Stiffy, for the base

19½"×12" (49.5×30.5 cm) piece of wool felt for the batting

1 package Mistyfuse fusible web

24" (61 cm) length of ½" (1.3 cm) wide grosgrain ribbon

1 charm (optional)

sketch in time
SKETCHBOOK WRAP

FINISHED SIZE *19.5" × 12" (49.5 × 30.5 cm)*

You can use this quilted sketchbook wrap pattern to make a cover for a book of almost any size. Because it's removable, you can re-use it each time you crack open a new sketchbook. Made in different sizes, this design would make a great cover for trashy novels, fresh notebooks, and themed photo albums.

Prepare the Materials

1 Cut the green fat quarter and one of the purple fat quarters down to 19½" × 12" (49.5 × 30.5 cm). Apply fusible web to the wrong sides of all of your fabric pieces, including the scraps for the letters and decorative stripes.

Create the Exterior

2 Fuse the 19½" × 12" (49.5 × 30.5 cm) piece of stiff interfacing to one side of the piece of wool felt. Fuse the green cover fabric to the other side of the wool felt batting.

3 Quilt the sketchbook wrap before you embellish it. I stitched random straight lines over the cover, but consider free-motion stitching waves or straight stitching a grid pattern.

Add the Embellishments

4 Use the no-reverse appliqué technique (page 25) to cut out the letters for the words "paint," "draw," and "sketch." Fuse them to the front side of the quilted wrap and then sew a single line of straight stitches through the center of each letter.

5 Cut six pieces of fabric from your scraps, each 1½" (3.8 cm) wide by 3" to 6" (7.5 to 15 cm) long. Fuse them along the right edge of the wrap to create uneven stripes, and then quilt them **(figure 1)**. I used straight stitches that echoed the outside shape of the stripes.

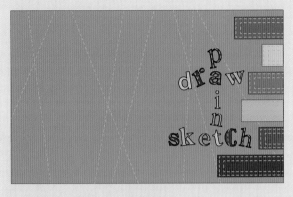

figure 1 - Fuse then stitch down the stripes and letters.

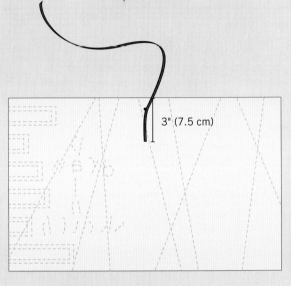

figure 2 - Stitch down a ribbon to the backside of the interfacing.

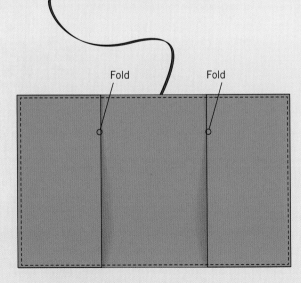

figure 3 - Attach the pockets to the lining.

Sew the Lining

6 Place the exterior of the 19½" × 12" (49.5 × 30.5 cm) sketchbook wrap wrong side up on your work surface. To attach a ribbon bookmark, pin one end of the 24" (61 cm) long ribbon to the center of the sleeve approximately 3" (7.5 cm) below the top edge **(figure 2)**.

7 Fuse the 19½" × 12" (49.5 × 30.5 cm) piece of purple lining fabric to the wrong side of the sketchbook wrap over the ribbon. Make sure that the long, unattached end of the ribbon stays out of the way.

8 From the remaining purple fat quarter, cut two 13" × 13" (35 × 35 cm) pieces for the pockets. Fold each of the pieces in half, wrong sides together, and press. These will be used to create the two inside sleeves that attach the sketchbook wrap to a book.

9 Pin the folded pocket pieces to the lining, right sides together, and match the raw outside edges. The folds of the sleeves should be facing toward the center of the sketchbook wrap. Stitch them in place where they attach to the lining, about ¼" (6 mm) away from the outside edges **(figure 3)**.

Finish the Edges

10 Set your sewing machine for a ¼" (6 mm) wide zig-zag stitch or a satin stitch. With straight stitches, sew around the edges of the sketchbook wrap to secure the lining to the cover and create a pretty, decorative finish on the edges.

11 If you wish, tie a charm to the loose end of the ribbon bookmark.

two quilted
color-block
THROW PILLOWS

My favorite style of pillow cover is an envelope-back pillow. It's fast and easy to make, and you can quickly pull the cover off of the pillow to wash it. I've designed two different fused fabric collage pillows, which would also be a great jumping-off point for making a wall hanging, a lap quilt, or even a bed-sized quilt.

supplies

PINWHEEL THROW PILLOW

¾ yd (68.5 cm) of light gray fabric for the pillow front and back

1 fat quarter of dark gray fabric for the outline strips

8 different 10" × 10" (25.5 × 25.5 cm) fabric scraps for the pillow front

19" × 19" (48.5 × 48.5 cm) piece of wool felt for the batting

1 package of Mistyfuse fusible web

Point turner

16" × 16" (40.5 × 40.5 cm) pillow form

WONKY SQUARE PILLOW

¾ yd (68.5 cm) of light gray fabric for the pillow front and back

1 fat quarter of dark gray fabric for the outline strips

8 to 12 different 10" × 10" (25.5 × 25.5 cm) fabric scraps for the wonky squares

19" × 19" (48.5 × 48.5 cm) piece of wool felt for the batting

1 package of Mistyfuse fusible web

Point turner

16" × 16" (40.5 × 40.5 cm) pillow form

Pinwheel Throw Pillow

Prepare the Front

1 Apply fusible web to all of your fabric scraps and to the dark gray fabric.

2 For the pillow front, cut a piece of light gray fabric 18" × 18" (45.5 × 45.5 cm). Mark the center line both horizontally and vertically with a chalk marker, dividing the square into quarters.

Add Two Layers of Rectangles

3 Cut four rectangles measuring 4" × 9" (10 × 23 cm), one from each of four different fabric scraps. Align them along the marked center line, with the short ends meeting in the center. Fuse them to the pillow front **(figure 1)**.

4 Pin the pillow front to the 19" × 19" (48.5 × 48.5 cm) piece of wool felt, right side up.

5 Quilt the rectangles and the gray sections. I used straight stitches and matching thread to quilt each section, repeating the longest edge of each shape.

6 Cut four smaller rectangles measuring 2" × 6" (5 × 15 cm), one each from the remaining different fabric scraps. Align them along the marked center lines and on top of the larger rectangles. Fuse them to the pillow front **(figure 2)**.

> **FABRIC COLLAGE TIP** *For your rectangles, choose highly contrasting colors so that they'll stand out against the light gray background. Or mix it up and use a printed fabric for the background and a solid fabric on the top of the stack of rectangles for even more visual contrast.*

7 Quilt the second layer of rectangles. I used straight stitches and matching thread to quilt each section and quilted the centermost smaller rectangles on the diagonal.

Outline the Rectangles

8 Cut outline strips from the dark gray fabric to fit the rectangles:

4 strips: ¼" × 2½" (6 mm × 6.5 cm)

4 strips: ¼" × 6½" (6 mm × 16.5 cm)

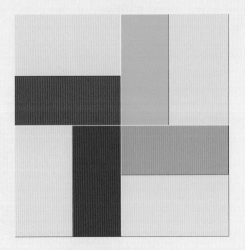

figure 1 - Create a pinwheel shape with rectangles.

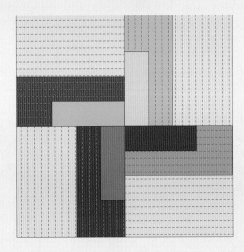

figure 2 - Layer a second set of smaller rectangles on top of the first pinwheel.

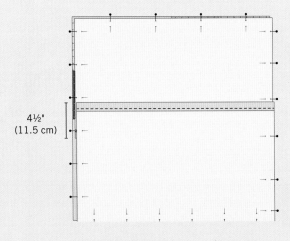

4½" (11.5 cm)

figure 3 - Pin the two back panels right sides together to create an envelope back.

4 strips: ¼" × 9" (6 mm × 23 cm)

2 strips: ¼" × 18" (6 mm × 45.5 cm)

9 Fuse the 2½" (6.5 cm) strips to the outside short edge of each small rectangle, allowing the ends of each strip to extend beyond the outside corners of the rectangles.

10 Fuse the 6½" (16.5 cm) strips to the long edge of each small rectangle. Allow the ends of each strip to overlap and extend past the outside corners of the rectangles.

11 Fuse the 9" (23 cm) strips to the long edge of the large rectangles. Again, allow the ends of each strip to extend beyond the outside corner of the rectangles.

12 Finish the outlines by fusing the two longest strips to the two centerlines that divide the four sections.

13 To secure the outlines, sew a single line of straight stitches through the center of all of the strips.

Assemble the Pillow

14 Trim the pillow front to measure 17" × 17" (43 × 43 cm).

15 Cut two back panels from the light gray fabric, each 17" × 12" (43 × 30.5 cm) for the pillow back.

16 With the right side up, hem one piece along one long side by folding up the edge 1" (2.5 cm) and pressing. Fold and press an additional 1" (2.5 cm) to the wrong side to enclose the raw edge.

Topstitch ½" (1.3 cm) from the folded edge.

Repeat with the second back panel.

17 Place the pillow front on your work surface, right side up. Layer the two hemmed pillow back pieces right sides together on the pillow front. Align all of the raw edges. The hemmed edges of the back panels should overlap by 4½" (11.5 cm) in the middle of the pillow (**figure 3**). Pin the three pieces together around the outside edges of the pillow.

Using a ½" (1.3 cm) seam allowance, stitch around all the edges.

18 Trim the corners diagonally to reduce bulk. Turn the pillow cover right side out, gently pushing out the corners with the point turner. Insert the pillow form.

5 ways
to make it your own

Think of these medium-size throw pillows as a jumping off point for any of your own design ideas. You can quickly sew them up in an afternoon to make your sofa more inviting or to liven up your bed linens.

You can experiment with your quilting scraps and new colors, and:

1 Use circles instead of wonky rectangles to fill the centers of the wonky squares.

2 Play with a combination of coordinating prints. The solid lines that outline each shape will provide a nice break for the eye between the print patterns.

3 Sew a line of decorative buttons to the top flap on the envelope back for some visual interest on the flipside of the pillow.

4 Add a decorative button to the inside of each wonky rectangle. Add a row of buttons to the inside of each smaller rectangle on the pinwheel pillow.

5 Amp up the whimsy in your pillows by sewing on some "Z's" using the no-reverse appliqué method (page 25) to create the letters.

Wonky Square Pillow

Create a Pattern

1 Cut a piece of paper 10"×10" (25.5×25.5 cm) and mark the center point. The easiest way to do this is to fold the paper in half, crease it, and then fold it in half again and crease it. Open the square and where the creases meet in the center is the center point. Number the sections from 1 to 4.

2 Divide the square into four uneven sections. Place the square of paper on your work surface and draw a diagonal line from the outside edge of section 1 to the outside edge of section 3, making sure that the line passes through the creased center point of the square **(figure 1)**. Begin drawing the horizontal line in section 1 at least 1½" (3.8 cm) away from the center of the top outside edge of the square.

3 Draw another diagonal line from the outside edge of section 2 to the outside edge of section 4, again making sure that the line passes through the creased center point of the square. Number the sections, and then cut the pattern apart on the drawn lines.

4 Apply fusible web to the wrong sides all of the fabric scraps for the wonky shapes.

Make the Front

5 Cut an 18"×18" (45.5×45.5 cm) square piece of light gray fabric for the pillow front. Using a chalk marker, divide the square into four equal sections and mark the center point.

6 Using your pattern pieces, cut sections 1 through 4 from four different pre-fused fabrics. Arrange them on the right side of the pillow front so that the sections match up at the center point. Fuse them in place.

7 Pin the pillow front right side up on the 19"×19" (48.5×48.5 cm) square of wool felt. Quilt the four wonky sections, making sure that you do not go beyond their outside edges.

I quilted straight stitches with threads that matched each of the four sections, using the long outside edges as a guide. The lines of stitching are spaced about ½" (1.3 cm) apart.

8 Cut four wonky shapes, one each from a different fabric and smaller than each of the four main sections. Roughly center one in each section, and then fuse them in place to the pillow front **(figure 2)**.

9 Quilt these four shapes with matching threads. Similar to the four main sections, quilt these wonky shapes with straight stitches that run perpendicular to one of the outside edges of the rectangle. Quilt your lines of stitches in different directions from one section to the next. This completes the first layer of wonky shapes.

10 Finally, from four different fabrics cut a second set of four wonky shapes, making them smaller than the first layer of shapes. Center them roughly in the middle of each of the first wonky shapes, and then fuse them in place **(figure 3)**.

11 Quilt these last four small shapes. Use matching thread and straight stitches, quilt in a direction different from the quilting in the rectangle below. All the rectangles are now in place.

Quilt the Background

12 To quilt the light gray background of the pillow front, sew lines of straight stitching ½" (1.3 cm) apart. Let the stitching overlap in the outside corner areas to create smaller squares.

QUILTING TIP *If you're worried about keeping your quilting lines straight, mark these stitching lines using a chalk marker and a ruler.*

Outline the Wonky Shapes

13 From the pre-fused dark gray fat quarter, cut eighteen strips that are ¼"×18" (6 mm×45.5 cm). You'll trim them to fit the outside edges of the four main sections and the wonky shapes on the pillow front.

14 Place long strips on each of the two diagonal lines that separate the four main sections. Trim the strips so that they don't extend past the outside edges of the 10"×10" (25.5×25.5 cm) square of fused rectangles.

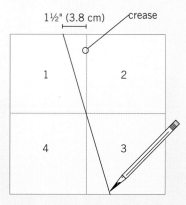

figure 1 - Draw a wonky square pattern.

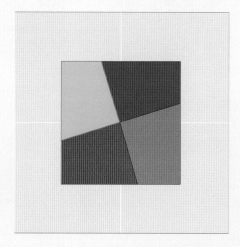

figure 2 - Fuse wonky squares to the center of the pillow.

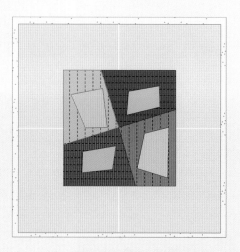

figure 3 - Fuse smaller wonky shapes on top of the quilted layer.

15 Outline all eight of the wonky shapes next. Trim the strips to fit your shapes, allowing each end to extend past the shape by ⅛" to ¼" (3 to 6 mm).

16 Add the last four long strips to the outside of the square, creating a frame around the square. Cut the strips about 11" (28 cm) long so that ½" (1.3 cm) extends past each side of the square.

17 To secure the outlines, sew a single line of straight stitches through the center of all of the dark gray strips.

Assemble the Pillow

18 Trim the pillow front to measure 17" × 17" (43 × 43 cm).

19 Cut two back panels from the light gray fabric, each 17" × 12" (43 × 30.5 cm), for the pillow back.

20 With one piece right side up, hem one 17" (43 cm) side by folding up the edge 1" (2.5 cm) to the wrong side and pressing. Fold and press an additional 1" (2.5 cm) to enclose the raw edge.

Topstitch ½" (1.3 cm) from the folded edge.

Repeat with the second back panel.

21 Place the pillow front on your work surface, right side up. Layer the two hemmed pillow back pieces right sides together on the pillow front. Align all of the raw edges. The hemmed edges should overlap by 4½" (11.5 cm) in the center of the pillow cover.

Pin the three pieces together around the outside edges of the pillow. Using a ½" (1.3 cm) seam allowance, stitch around all of the edges **(figure 3, page 130)**.

22 Trim the corners diagonally to reduce bulk. Turn the pillow cover right side out, gently pushing out the corners with a point turner. Insert the pillow form.

fused
log
cabin
LAP QUILT

supplies

2¼ yd (2.3 m) of light gray fabric for the quilt top background

1 yd (91.5 cm) of dark gray fabric for the blocks and the binding

8 different ½ yd (45.5 cm) pieces of fabric for the blocks

5 yd (4.6 m) of coordinating fabric for the backing

2 packages of Mistyfuse fusible web

50" × 84" (127 × 213 cm) piece of low-loft batting

Walking foot for your sewing machine (optional)

FINISHED SIZE *42" × 76" (106.5 × 193 cm)*

I love the look of a traditional log cabin block, but I hate doing all of the short bursts of sewing and endless seam pressing. So, I came up with an easy fused version. As this quilt shows, fusing can be used for so much more than just creating quilts to hang on the wall! A fused quilt goes together so much faster and can be just as functional as its pieced counterpart, as long as you anchor the fused pieces with stitching.

Prepare Fabric Strips

1 Cut a 10" (25.5 cm) wide piece along the length of the dark gray fabric and reserve it for the border.

Apply fusible web to the wrong sides of the remaining dark gray fabric and each of the eight contrasting colors.

2 Cut fifteen 2" × 2" (5 × 5 cm) squares from the pre-fused dark gray fabric for the centers of the blocks. For a wonky look like my quilt, cut the squares a bit off kilter.

FABRIC COLLAGE TIP *Don't cut all of the strips for the log cabin blocks evenly. Cut them at an angle so that one end is slightly wider than the other. Uneven widths will make your finished blocks even wonkier.*

3 Cut all of the fabric pieces for the logs into strips that measure 1" to 1½" (2.5 to 3.8 cm) wide and the length of the fabric.

Fuse the Log Cabin Blocks

4 Cover your ironing surface with a nonstick pressing sheet. Place one center square piece on the ironing surface right side up. This is piece 1 **(figure 1)**.

5 Fuse a strip of colored fabric to one side of the center square, overlapping the edges by ⅛" to ¼" (3 mm to 6 mm). This is piece 2. Trim it so that the outside edges match the center square **(figure 2)**.

6 Fuse another strip of colored fabric across the edge of piece 1 and piece 2, overlapping the edges by ⅛" (3 mm). This is piece 3. Trim to match the outside edges **(figure 3)**.

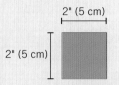

figure 1 - Start with a square as the center of the block.

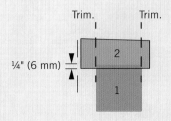

figure 2 - Add one wonky strip to the top of the center, then trim to fit.

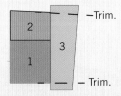

figure 3 - Fuse a second wonky strip, then trim to fit.

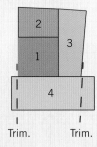

figure 4 - Fuse another wonky strip to the bottom of the square, then trim to fit.

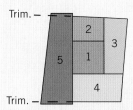

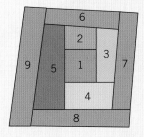

figure 5 - Complete the square with a final wonky strip, then trim to fit.

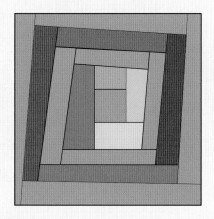

figure 6 - Finish the first set of squares with a gray border.

figure 7 - Your finished block should measure at least 10" x 10" (25.5 × 25.5 cm).

7 Fuse another strip of colored fabric across the edge of piece 1 and piece 3, overlapping the edges by ⅛" (3 mm). This is piece 4. Trim to match the outside edges **(figure 4)**.

8 Fuse one last strip of colored fabric across the edge of piece 4, piece 1, and piece 2, overlapping the edges by ⅛" (3 mm). This is piece 5. Trim to match the outside edges **(figure 5)**.

9 Finally, fuse four strips of dark gray fabric around the edges of the block, following the same steps to add the colored strips around the center block **(figure 6)**.

10 Following the same steps, add one more round of four colored strips and one more round of dark gray strips **(figure 7)**.

Your finished block should measure at least 10"×10" (25.5×25.5 cm). I like to make my blocks a little larger and then trim them down to size.

11 Repeat the steps above to make fifteen blocks, each measuring 10"×10" (25.5×25.5 cm).

> **DESIGN TIP** *The finished quilt size is 44"×76" (112×193 cm), which is a very generous size for a lap quilt. If you want to make your quilt smaller, just start with a smaller background fabric size and make your blocks a little smaller. To make the quilt larger, simply increase the number and size of the blocks and the amount of background fabric.*

Fuse the Quilt Top

12 Cut both selvedge edges off of the light gray background fabric so that it measures 42" (106.5 cm) wide. Then cut the length of the piece of fabric to measure 76" (193 cm). You will have a rectangle measuring 42" × 76" (106.5 × 193 cm).

13 Arrange your fifteen fused blocks into five rows with three blocks in each row. The three blocks in each row should be spaced 2½" (9.5 cm) apart, leaving 3½" (9 cm) on each outside edge of the background. The five blocks in each column should be spaced about 3½" (9 cm) apart, leaving 4" (10 cm) on the top and bottom edges of the background.

> **PIECING TIP** *If you've increased the number of blocks to make a larger quilt and don't have background fabric wide enough to fit all of the blocks, just sew two lengths of fabric right sides together using a ¼" (6 mm) seam. Press the seam open and then fuse your blocks on top.*

When you're happy with the arrangement of the blocks, fuse them in place to the background.

Create the Quilt Sandwich

14 Cut the backing fabric into two pieces each measuring 25" × 84" (63.5 × 213 cm). Using a ¼" (6 mm) seam allowance, stitch the two pieces right sides together along the 84" (213 cm) edges to create a backing that is a bit wider than required. Press the seam allowances open.

With the wrong side facing up, smooth the backing on your work surface—or floor—to remove all of the wrinkles. Place strips (or scraps) of fusible web on the backing. Use your nonstick pressing sheet and press with a hot iron to fuse the strips in place.

15 Center the 50" × 84" (127 × 213 cm) piece of batting on top of the pre-fused backing fabric. Press to fuse the two layers together. With the batting facing up, place strips (or scraps) of fusible web on top. Use your pressing sheet and press with a hot iron to fuse them in place.

16 Place the quilt top on top of the batting, smoothing out any wrinkles, working from the center of the quilt top to the outer edges, and then press with a hot iron to fuse to the batting. This will keep the quilt top from shifting while you quilt.

Add Quilting

17 Keep the quilting pattern simple so that the colorful blocks are the focal point. To quilt in the same manner I did, use a ruler and a chalk marker to mark vertical and horizontal quilting lines on the light gray fabric only. Start quilting 1" (2.5 cm) away from the outside of the dark gray borders of your blocks and space the lines of stitches about 1" (2.5 cm) apart.

18 Begin quilting the background, working your way from the center of the quilt toward the outside edges.

Use a walking foot if you have one. This ensures that the layers of the quilt sandwich will feed evenly and keep the fabric from puckering while you sew.

19 To quilt the log cabin blocks like I did, use a narrow zigzag stitch on the outside edges of the blocks. Also, zigzag stitch on the edges between each of the colored and dark gray strips to secure the overlapping edges.

Finish the Quilt

20 When you are done quilting, square up and trim the edges to measure 41" × 76" (104 × 193 cm). Cut four strips from the lengthwise edge of the dark gray fabric that you reserved for the binding.

21 Following the directions in Chapter 6, sew on the binding. Because this quilt will see more wear and tear as a sofa throw, secure the binding by hand stitching it to the back of the quilt.

5 ways to make it your own

A wonky log cabin quilt can be made in so many different ways! You can make it more or less wonky simply by changing how drastically diagonal you cut your center blocks and your strips.

Even more dramatic are the color choices you make. You could personalize your quilt if you:

1 Lighten the colors in this quilt—use white as the background instead of gray.

2 Swap in a variety of batik fabrics instead of solid colors.

3 Make an ombre version of this log cabin quilt that uses fifteen different colors—assign a range of shades of one color for each block.

4 Put together a super luxe version using only silk fabrics instead of quilting cottons.

5 Make your quilt top using blocks in different sizes. Place them randomly over the quit top instead of in a grid pattern. Or, for a different look, place the blocks on point by rotating them 90 degrees.

ABOUT THE
Contributors

I asked these nine very gifted artists to contribute to my book so you could see how versatile and innovative fusing can be. Although we've all used the same fusing technique and fusible web to construct our quilts, we've achieved very different results. Our own personal styles shine through in each one.

Deborah Boschert creates art quilts and fiber collages that are rich in texture, dimension, and imagery. They often include personal symbols such as houses, leaves, stones, and handwriting. Her art quilt *Windows Arise* is on page 28. *deborahsstudio.com.*

Jamie Fingal is known as the "Rebel Quilter." Her style is eclectic, edgy, and whimsical. Her philosophy on making quilts is more about having fun than achieving perfection. She uses vibrant colors, shapes, and textures to create artwork that invites the viewer in for a closer look. Her art quilt *work original* is on page 37. *jamiefingaldesigns.blogspot.com.*

Barb Forrister's true love is creating nature and pictorial scenes in a three-dimensional manner. An avid environmentalist and recycler, Barb gets her inspiration from observing nature and employing unusual and upcycled materials to convey textural surfaces. Her art quilt *Mystique* is on page 46. *barbforrister.com.*

Leslie Tucker Jenison is inspired by the textural beauty found in the patterns of natural and human-made environments. She loves the tactile experience of working with cloth and paper and using dye, paint, and thread to create unique imagery on these surfaces. Her art quilt *Labels* is on page 41. *leslietuckerjenison.blogspot.com.*

Desiree Habicht is a multimedia artist and instructor who works in fine art, fiber art, and commercial art. She designs fabric and quilt patterns for the quilting industry. Her artwork also appears on commercial products. Her art quilt *The Sunbather* is on page 57. *desireehabicht.com.*

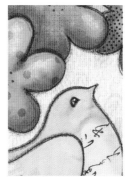

Terri Stegmiller creates whimsical art quilts that vibrate with color and energy. She finds inspiration in her surroundings and loves to include images of flowers, cats, and the female face in her work. Her art quilt *Flower Gazing* is on page 49. *terristegmiller.com.*

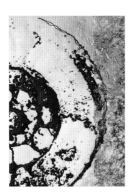

Lyric Kinard is an award-winning artist who creates quilts that attempt to uplift the viewer and make a statement about the role of women, about the world around us and our place in it, or about something that's just plain lovely to look at. Her art quilt *Ammonite VIII* is on page 31. *lyrickinard.com.*

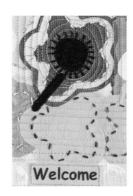

Kathy York's interest in fabric design began as an extension of surface design on her art quilts. Many of her designs originate from found objects that are used for batik. Her work is well known for its bright, fresh colors and bold, crisp graphics. Her art quilt *Welcome* is on page 55. *aquamoonartquilts.blogspot.com.*

Kathy Sperino is a professional long-arm quilter who draws on her love of nature to inspire much of her work. Using mixed-media techniques coupled with traditional quilting techniques, Kathy creates quilts that draw you in for a closer look. Her art quilt *Purple Reeds* is on page 21. *finishinglinesbyksperino.blogspot.com.*

Resources

Fabric dyeing supplies
Pro Chemical and Dye
prochemicalanddye.com

Dharma Trading
dharmatrading.com

Prepared for dye fabrics
Test Fabrics
testfabrics.com

Hand-dyed solid fabrics
Cherrywood Fabrics
cherrywoodfabrics.com

Vicki Welsh Hand Dyed Fabrics
etsy.com/shop/vickiwelsh

Batik and cotton fabric
Hoffman Fabric
hoffmanfabrics.com

**Mistyfuse fusible web, Goddess
Teflon pressing sheet, and
Transdoodle chalk transfer paper**
Mistyfuse
mistyfuse.com

Threads
Superior Threads
superiorthreads.com

Gutermann
guetermann.com

Aurifil
aurifil.com

Interfacing
Peltex 70
pellonprojects.com

Timtex
ctpub.com

Stiffy
longcreekmills.com

Textile foil
Laura Murray Designs
lauramurraydesigns.com

Metal leaf
Dick Blick Art Materials
dickblick.com

Iron-off chalk
Sue Pelland Designs
suepellanddesigns.com

Die cutters
Accuquilt
accuquilt.com

Big Shot
sizzix.com

Handbag supplies
Erica's Purse Tote and Bag Notions
ericas.com

Tall Poppy Hand Bag Supplies
tallpoppycraft.com

Serrated blade scissors
Havel's Sewing
havelssewing.com

Needles
Schmetz Needles
schmetzneedles.com

Thermofax silk screen designs:
Terri Stegmiller Art & Design
etsy.com/shop/TerriStegmillerArt

Lyric Kinard Thermofax
lyrickinard.com

Marcy Tilton Silk Screens
marcytilton.com

Index

Take your fabric art to the next level with these new and inspiring books from Interweave.

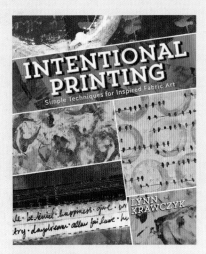
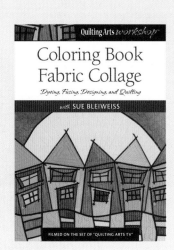